GERMAN MILWAUKEE

ITS HISTORY - ITS RECIPES

BY

TRUDY KNAUSS PARADIS

WITH E. J. BRUMDER

EDITED BY

ROBIN PARADIS-KENT

G. BRADLEY PUBLISHING, INC. • ST. LOUIS, MISSOURI 63122

PUBLICATION STAFF

Authors: ....Trudy Knauss Paradis

....E. J. Brumder

Editor: ....Robin Paradis-Kent

Book Design: ....Diane Kramer

Color Photography ....Katherine Bish

Photo Design ....Michael Bruner

Dust Jacket Design ....Michael Bruner

Copy Editor ....Diane Gannon

Publisher: ....G. Bradley Publishing, Inc.

THIS PUBLICATION WAS SPONSORED BY THE MILWAUKEE TURNERS

Rose Marie Barber

The publication staff is extremely thankful to the Milwaukee Turners and its Executive Director Rose Marie Barber. Mrs. Barber passed away in September 2006. She was instrumental in the development and production of *German Milwaukee: Its History – Its Recipes*.

DEDICATION

It is with overwhelming pride for our German ancestors that we dedicate this book to the early immigrants whose indomitable spirit led them to embark on a new life; leaving their home, friends, and family. After overcoming all the odds against them, they not only bettered their own lives; they have ultimately enriched ours and, indeed, the City of Milwaukee.

Katherine Bish

A graduate of Eastern Illinois School of Journalism, Katherine Bish has been telling her stories through pictures since 1998. Her food photography has appeared in *St. Louis Magazine*, *Sauce Magazine*, and the *St. Louis Post-Dispatch*. Her work is featured in the 2005 publication *Greektown Chicago: Its History – Its Recipes*.

ISBN 0-9774512-1-6
Printed in the U.S.A.

Please check the G. Bradley Publishing web site to review other Midwest history books such as this:
www.gbradleypublishing.com

TABLE OF CONTENTS

Herzlich Willkommen! . . . . *Heartfelt Welcome!*

FOREWORD

"Our ship docked in the harbor. There was no pier. In the distance we saw a few houses. Is this truly Milwaukee? Three months had passed since we began our journey. Just then we were lowered into small boats which took us and all our belongings to shore. Sitting on our featherbeds and cases, we waited while Papa went into town to secure lodgings for the night. Luckily, he found rooms and, in the chilly night air, we all hurried as best we could on the wet sand. Then, to bed on dry land. *Gute Nacht!* So began our adventure in our new homeland.

We were among thousands of immigrants who sought more space and larger opportunities for themselves and their children. Milwaukee was Wisconsin's most promising village with pleasant surroundings and climate. It reminded us of home."

Grüss Gott . . . . *Hello*

The swift passage of time often erases knowledge of the past and with that loss a lack of understanding why things are the way they are today, and what gave rise to them. In contemporary Wisconsin, the impact of the arrival of people from many different world cultures tends to obscure the knowledge of earlier immigrants who contributed greatly to the foundation of present-day society. In Wisconsin in the 19th and 20th centuries many German immigrants and people from German-speaking lands contributed heavily to the kind of culture that currently exists in the state. And it is important, therefore, from time to time to try to recall these contributions.

During the 19th century, there was a very large migration of people from German states to North America, South America, and Australia. They came in waves, so to speak. One wave came to the interior of the continent by way of the Hudson and Mohawk Rivers and the Great Lakes. Another wave went along the Ohio River Valley. Still another traveled up the Mississippi River from the Caribbean and a sizeable group even went to Texas.

The German immigrants to Wisconsin in the 1820s and 1840s encountered an American Indian culture which was a hunting and gathering culture. The migrants themselves were farmers and builders. Within two decades, they had constructed substantial cities and villages. Milwaukee, for example, by 1850 became known as the "German Athens on Lake Michigan" because of its advanced culture.

At present in Wisconsin, the evidence of the cultural influence of Germans is widespread. It is found in high architecture, in residential and commercial buildings, in churches and government buildings, in harbors, railroads, and airports. German immigrants conducted formal schools, influenced museums and libraries, contributed to higher education, built hospitals and homes to care for children and the aged. They developed singing and musical instrumental groups, they supported drama, and they were writers and publishers. Germans were also advanced in painting and the arts.

Germans developed theologians and philosophers and even writers of scholarly works of many kinds. The evidence of the activity of the immigrants from German states is strongest in the eastern counties of Wisconsin, and also Marathon County, but now persons descended from these immigrants are spread throughout the state and nation.

Of special interest is the influence of the Germanic peoples on the formation of ideas about social welfare and later corresponding legislation, and the protection of the disadvantaged. Our country's social security system, for example, has direct Germanic roots.

The more recent flow of immigrants from Germany and German-speaking lands has brought engineers and technicians to the state, who are making the local industries competitive through their skills in manufacturing, business, and design. Germans also were active in the conservation movement in both the state and the nation.

The decline in the teaching of proficiency in the German language and in reading German must be now considered a weakness in United States' education, especially because of the developments in science, industry, geology, and religion emerging in the states. There's a current need in the United States for people of learning who can tap these newly developing sources of information.

This book presents important information on the past positive activities of people from German-speaking lands, and is useful, therefore, for many Wisconsin residents who have some German ancestry and for persons generally interested in the important facts of history that have been obscured by time. A fresh study of the German roots of Wisconsin life will prove immensely enriching for those who engage in it.

Frank P. Zeidler

Frank P. Zeidler
September 5, 2005
Milwaukee, Wisconsin

Born of Austrian parents in Milwaukee, Frank P. Zeidler [1912 - 2006] served as Mayor of Milwaukee from 1948-1960. He and his devoted wife, Agnes, had six children, the youngest of whom followed in his footsteps and is currently Mayor of Williamsburg, Virginia.

Zeidler had "…integrity, energy and principles …was a human encyclopedia of Milwaukee history; kept meticulous records of everything he did; had impeccable integrity; depth, sincerity; intellectual ability; was a 'peace person'; was the last living link with a legendary period of Milwaukee's history; a pivotal figure who embodied honest and efficient government; gave a voice to those who had none; had inspiring leadership; left a lasting impact; always believed public service was a noble and life-long calling; loved the city and was loved by its citizens; had no mundane, selfish motives; was a sincere and big-hearted man; with fierce idealism; a model Milwaukeean; an authentic American hero." Senators, Congressmen, Mayors, historians, journalists, friends — all said similar things about former Mayor Frank Zeidler.

A young Frank Zeidler celebrates his election as mayor of Milwaukee in 1948.

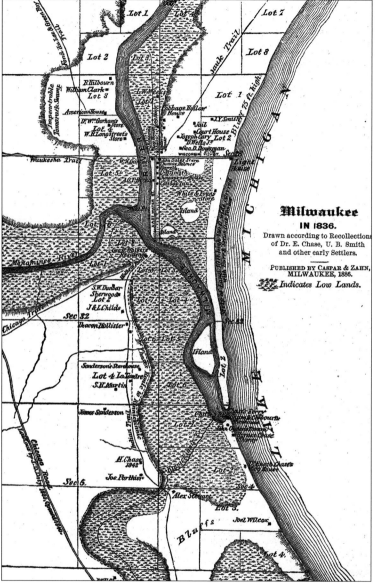

Milwaukee
IN 1836.
Drawn according to Recollections
of Dr. E. Chase, U. B. Smith
and other early Settlers.

PUBLISHED BY CASPAR & ZAHN,
MILWAUKEE, 1886.
Indicates Low Lands.

Wilhelm Strothmann

The first German immigrant settled in Milwaukee County in 1835. Wilhelm Strothmann walked from Chicago with all of his possessions on his back and settled in Greenfield Township. Twelve hundred Germans came to the village each week in the 1840s, and in 1843, the Town of Milwaukee was formed. By 1859, Germans made up one-third of the local population. It is said that they were recognized by their long beards, heavy coats, broad-visored caps and arm-long tobacco pipes, as well as their patience, skill, and endurance. They were energetic, hardy, and persevering.

Poor conditions at home motivated some German immigrants, while a thirst for adventure attracted others to the New World. Indeed, Henry Bleyer, a wood-turner from Hanover, left his family to the comforts of Detroit until he had built a home for them. One family walked from Michigan City, Indiana, along Lake Michigan's sand beaches while pulling a boat full of their belongings. However, mostly bachelors initially came to the settlement, among them craftsmen, who were welcomed for their skills, and would-be farmers who passed through to the frontier.

Small bands of Indian tribes here included Potawatomi, Menomonee, Chippewa, Fox, Sauk, and Winnebago. "Milwaukee" in Indian language is thought to mean "Gathering Place by the Waters." Pictured is a teepee-inspired invitation from the Milwaukee Carnival Association to its "First Grand Ball at the New Public Library & Museum Building, Friday Eve, July 1, 1898."

The Federal Government held the Green Bay Land Sale of former Indian Lands bordering Lake Michigan in 1835. Milwaukee, part of that land sale, was the best port on the western shore of the lake. Three rivers divided the marshy land that was to become Milwaukee, namely: the Milwaukee, Menomonee, and the Kinnickinnic. Three settlers, Solomon Juneau, Byron Kilbourn, and George Walker, each bought 160 acres at $1.25 per acre. Juneau developed his town between the Milwaukee River and Lake Michigan. Kilbourn developed his town west of the Milwaukee River, while George Walker's Point was on high ground south of the Menomonee River.

Guten Morgen . . . . . .

THE NEW LAND

Alive with fresh ideas of how things should be, but with little actual freedom at home, many Germans sailed away from their native land so that they might create a German state to suit themselves. They yearned for freedom from low wages, repeated military service, and unproductive soil. They wanted to escape the constant threat of war, hunger, religious intolerance, and repressed dissent.

However, other German immigrants hoped that their children could become one with the citizens of this country. Carl Schurz, of the Liberal Republican movement in the 1870s, was a beloved German scholar and statesman. One of the most important German-Americans of the 19th Century, Schurz explained that, "Germans are not called upon to form a separate nationality but rather to contribute to the American nationality."

The first large wave of German immigration began in the 1830s. Generally, those who emigrated were not impoverished, but they arrived with rising expectations to better their economic status, coming with their own money, ability, and will.

Another wave came in 1848, following the failure of democratic revolutions in Europe. Comprising ten percent of German-speaking newcomers, these were people of high intellect, many of them wealthy and cultured. Moreover, although this group would eventually become very politically influential in America, they continued to observe Old World customs and diversions such as German beer gardens, the Turner organizations, singing societies, the German Theater, and coffee houses.

When the U.S. Government assumed control of immigration in 1855, many German immigrants landed in New York at Castle Garden on the southern tip of Manhattan.

Chicago also became a prominent immigrant destination. Its strategic location at the southern tip of Lake Michigan also contributed to the city becoming a major rail transportation hub. Yet, many immigrants opted for the more scenic area around Milwaukee with its moraines, ravines, kettles, and kames. The high bluffs around the marshy river land provided scenic views of Lake Michigan and the countryside. It reminded them of home in Germany.

Later, many immigrants came because there were too many mouths to feed at home. In the German States, land had been subdivided by inheritance and often could not support a family. When Wisconsin became a state in 1848, the state sent promoters to Germany with fliers advertising climate and culture to attract settlers.

The Germans came in great numbers, leaving from Bremerhaven, Hamburg, and Le Havre. After several weeks on a sailing ship or a steamship, they reached America, landing after 1892 on Ellis Island. They traveled up the Hudson River to Albany and moved slowly west on the Erie Canal to the Great Lakes. After mid-century they might have taken trains at least part of the way.

Wisconsin lands were for sale, and letters back to Germany praised the region for its opportunities. The advantages of a large German-speaking population also made it easier for a newcomer to adjust to the American surroundings.

The first Germans to come in a group passed through Milwaukee in 1839. This migration started when 400 families left Pomerania because King Frederick Wilhelm III of Prussia had decreed that all Lutherans must worship in the State's Reformed churches. Most of these Old Lutherans (*Die Alte Lutheraner*) settled in Buffalo, New York, but 39 families came through Milwaukee and settled together about 20 miles north in Ozaukee County. They called their church and town center *Freistadt* (Free Town). The original cemetery remains today, but their church has been rebuilt several times.

The village economy after the Green Bay Land sale in 1835 was one of boom to 1837, then bust to 1842. Land speculation fueled the fever so that lot prices could double in one day. The financial panic of 1837 in the

Mecklenburgische Colonie bei Milwaukee.

Mecklenburgers settled on the south side of Milwaukee, in the Fifth Ward. Another area close by was known by its nickname, "The Wooden Shoe District." While today we view "wooden shoes" as being predominantly Dutch, many Europeans, including Germans, wore wooden shoes. Yet another area, called "Bavarian Heaven," also was located in old Milwaukee.

View of Milwaukee west of the river where most Germans lived in 1886. Germans concentrated in settlements based on their home provinces and religious backgrounds. They settled northwest in Kilbourntown on hard ground which became known as Gartenstadt *(Garden Town) so named for its little homes with fenced-in gardens displaying lovely flowers. To the rear of the houses were little vegetable plots.*

Guten Nachmittag ......

United States made paper money useless. After several years of heated argument, the three original settlements, Juneautown, Kilbourntown and Walkers Point joined to form the City of Milwaukee in 1846 after receiving permission from the Territory of Wisconsin. Two years later, in 1848, Wisconsin Territory became a state.

Lumberjacks felled the forests of Wisconsin, and others milled lumber, built houses and other buildings. On the cleared lands, farmers planted wheat, an easy crop. Flour mills ground wheat with water power from the Milwaukee River. Speculators traded Wisconsin's fine grain crops in the Grain Exchange Room of the Chamber of Commerce building. During the Civil War, Milwaukee was the largest exporter of wheat in the world. Then the cinch bug attacked for two summers in a row and discouraged replanting. Also, the fertility of the soil declined and farmers turned to raising dairy cattle. There were always retail butchers but wholesale meat packing presented important opportunities. The raw materials for tanning the animal hides were here, in that tamarack trees grew in the marshes, thereby providing tanbark for the many tanneries, owned mostly by German-Americans.

There was a short flurry of canal building, but the city fathers realized that

The New Coeln House of 1850, on the stagecoach route between Milwaukee and Racine, presently advertises itself as Milwaukee's oldest tavern and is called "Landmark 1850 Inn." Coeln (Köln) refers to Cologne, Germany.

In the 1880s, the main German shopping area was located west of the Milwaukee River. The German settlers continued to move north and west from downtown. Another core group of Germans lived in and around the Market Square area, east of the river. The English-speaking settlers, who had come from the East Coast, Ireland and England, were called Yankees, and they lived east of the river as well.

CIVIL WAR

Above: In 1876 this South Side Rifle Team posed at South Side Turnhall. The rifle club was the forerunner of the State Militia. The three German militia groups, German Green Jaegers, German Black Jaegers and Milwaukee Light Guard, stood firmly behind the Wisconsin anti-slavery laws. The 26th Wisconsin Infantry Regiment in the Civil War was known as the German Regiment.

Right: One of these men is William Steinmeyer, who started a large Milwaukee grocery establishment, Steinmeyer's. He re-enlisted many times and became a Captain in the 26th Wisconsin Infantry.

Left: A marble memorial for the Milwaukee Turner Volunteers who died in the Civil War can be seen when visiting the Milwaukee Turner Hall. One can find it on the landing of the stairway leading up to the Turner Ballroom.

Guten Tag . . . .

railroads would bring future prosperity. Eventually Milwaukee would have two nationally important rail companies: The Chicago, Milwaukee, St. Paul, & Pacific Line and the Chicago & Northwestern. As such, settlers in the hinterland were eventually well connected to the City of Milwaukee.

Though Milwaukee was to become famous for German-American breweries, ironically, the first Milwaukee brewery was established by Welshmen, but in the 1840s Germans started producing beer of their own. This industry soon achieved impressive growth, not only because of the natural German preference for beer, but also due to the fact that Milwaukee produced good beer, a product that began to be sold nationally after Milwaukee supplied Chicago with beer following the Great Fire of 1871.

Milwaukee was, and still is, a bustling city of commerce and industry. It was once the world's largest primary wheat market, a center of leather tanning, and the world capital for beer. Germans worked hard; their businesses included restaurants, meat markets, bakeries, dairies, taverns, outdoor markets, machine shops, foundries and printing facilities. German was spoken at many retail outlets which provided clothing, hardware, and furniture – some even displayed signs saying

This early Jahrmarkt *was a gathering, held annually at the end of summer or early fall, where farmers brought their produce to the city and celebrated the harvest.*

Hinkel's Saloon, on the corner of 3rd and (now) State streets, was a large, busy establishment at the turn of the century. John Hinkel worked at the Best Brewery for a time; he then opened his own saloon and eatery in 1877.

"English Spoken Here."

Politically, Wisconsin was an anti-slavery state. Feelings ran high at the time, but a federal law stated that escaped slaves must be returned to their masters. No German group or militia sided with the federal government on this issue.

While Post-Civil War America rebuilt itself, political upheaval began anew in Europe. Prussia under Bismarck promoted the Wars of Unification against Austria, Denmark, and France. As a result of the Franco-Prussian War in 1871, the German Empire was founded. The many Kingdoms, Duchies, Grand Duchies, Principalities, and Free Hanseatic Cities were a hodgepodge of about 300 small states that became the new Germany. Nationalism and pride followed in due course. This development boosted the concept of *Klein Deutschland* (Small Germany) in America, and it retarded the process of Americanization. In Milwaukee the prideful Germans were the dominant ethnic group; over the years this probably helped the Yankees and other citizens to accept other ethnic groups in the city. German, Polish, and Norwegians show double digit percentages of the state population today. All the other ethnic groups, which number more than 60, show single digit percentages.

Carl Schurz, an extraordinary statesman, who helped elect Lincoln and served as the 13th U.S. Secretary of the Interior (1877-1881), said at the opening of the Chicago World's Fair in 1893, "I have always been in favor of a healthy Americanization, but that does not mean a complete disavowal of our German heritage. It means that our character should take on the best of that which is American, and combine it with the best of

A typical grocery delivery wagon is shown here before the advent of automobiles.

The freeways of the early 19th century were the rivers and lakes. Milwaukee had the best port on the western shore of Lake Michigan. Men worked hard on the docks loading and unloading merchandise from the ships. The hope of Milwaukee was to become the preeminent trans-shipment point in the Midwest, but railroad connections made Chicago into the most important hub.

that which is German. By doing this, we can best serve the American people and their civilization."

In 1890, German language newspapers had twice the circulation of English language papers. The "Germania" papers led the political debate against the Bennett Law, which stated that English was required in public and private classrooms. The German-Americans and other immigrant groups were angry at the assault on their culture and voted out all the Republicans in Madison and in Congress.

German-Americans also largely ignored the other main provision of the law, namely, that all children be required to attend school, due to their belief that the intended purpose of this provision was to swiftly assimilate and Americanize their children.

Milwaukee was strongly German in spirit, but that was to change.

Frederick Poehlmann established his bakery on Ogden and Jackson in 1853. German immigrants missed their rye bread, so Poehlmann walked to Cedarburg (a town 17 miles north of Milwaukee) and brought back rye flour in a wagon pulled by a team of oxen. The trip took three days!

This newspaper advertised Singer Sewing Machines, butchering utensils, Blatz Beer, cigars, bells, wine, liquor, feathers and feather beds – all in German.

The well-established German Stock Company performed in old Market Hall (at right) and then moved to the Stadt Theater on 3rd Street. After their move from Market Hall, some city offices were located there.

Architect Henry C. Koch, designed the 1893 Milwaukee City Hall in the German Renaissance Revival Style. Other designs by the prolific architect are the Milwaukee Turners' Hall, 4th Street School (the Golda Meir School), the Pfister Hotel, the Ward Theater at Soldier's Home (Wood, Wisconsin), and Grace Lutheran Church.

Originally surrounded by wigwams in 1837, this house (below) is in Market Square, a small German settlement east of the river. It was owned by Matthias Stein, Milwaukee's first gunsmith, who came to Milwaukee from Germany via many American cities. While in Washington D.C., he took daily walks with an elderly gentleman who questioned him about conditions in Germany. Later, when he inquired who this interested man was, he was told, "Why, that's President Andy Jackson!"

The 1893 foundation of the present City Hall (at left) consists of 2,584 cedar poles which were driven into the marshy land along the Milwaukee River. The tower houses a ten-ton bell. Installation took Henry Buestrin's crew one week to complete with ropes, horses, and pulleys. The Romanesque arches and Flemish gables mimic German architecture. Many architects in Milwaukee at that time were schooled in Germany.

Guten Abend......

Milling, along with tanning and brewing, were the three major early industries in Milwaukee following the arrival of the Germans. They ground barley to be malted for beer, wheat and rye for bread flour, along with corn, flax, and oats.

Grain elevators were located on the banks of the Milwaukee River for ease of loading and unloading grain on Lake Michigan ships. Wheat traveled to London, England in 77 days.

Grist mills processed farmers' products into ready income. Initially, animals or water pow-ered mill operations; later, steam replaced these systems. This flour mill, located on South Water Street, was Milwaukee's first steam-powered mill.

This flour and feed store (above) was located on Green Bay Road. Today, celebrating 200 miles of living history, the State of Wisconsin has posted markers so that Wisconsin's Ethnic Settlement Trail can be followed. (W.E.S.T. was founded in 1989 by Carol Rittenhouse and Alan Pape) This former Indian trail became a military road in 1834 from Fort Dearborn in Chicago to Fort Howard in Green Bay. The largest nineteenth-century immigrant group – the Germans – consisted of 15 sub-groups in settlements along the Lake Michigan shoreline, living along this Green Bay Road trail. The largest German groups came from Pomerania, Saxony, Hessen (Hunsruckers), Bavaria, and Mecklenburg. "Green Bay Road acts as a cultural thread in a necklace of ethnic jewels."

GERMAN CHURCHES

In 1845, most German immigrants were Catholic. Many came from the Rhineland. The first Catholic Church in the settlement was St. Peter's, and that small building is now at Old World Wisconsin, an open-air historical museum. The German Catholics built old St. Mary's. When Swiss-born Bishop John Martin Henni was sent to Milwaukee, he conducted Mass in Latin and German. Further, he requested the Catholic Church in Germany to send the religious orders of the Sisters of Notre Dame and the School Sisters of St. Francis to teach the German language to schoolchildren. Bishop Henni founded St. Francis Seminary, which is the oldest Catholic seminary in the Midwest and became a center of German Catholic thought. Sister Caroline of the Sisters of Notre Dame opened the first German church school "in the wild," west of the Alleghenies in the basement of old St. Mary's.

The Lutherans split over doctrine, and churches developed separately: St. Paul's Lutheran Church; *Dreieinigkeits Kirche* (Trinity Church) Missouri Synod; *Gnaden Kirche* (Grace Lutheran Church) Wisconsin Synod; later in

St. Mary's Church is the city's oldest German Roman Catholic Church. King Ludwig of Bavaria donated to the parish the painting of the Annunciation hanging above the ornately carved altar. The stained glass windows, Stations of the Cross, the altar, and all of the carved wooden statues came from the Franz Meyer studio in Munich, Germany. The interior was renovated in 1982 and keeps its traditional German appearance.

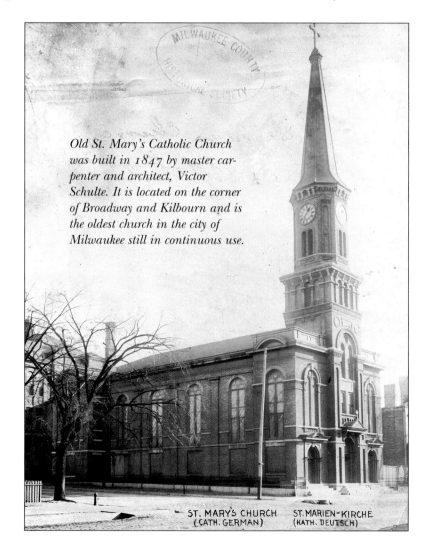

Old St. Mary's Catholic Church was built in 1847 by master carpenter and architect, Victor Schulte. It is located on the corner of Broadway and Kilbourn and is the oldest church in the city of Milwaukee still in continuous use.

ST. MARY'S CHURCH (CATH. GERMAN) ST. MARIEN-KIRCHE (KATH. DEUTSCH)

1890, Redeemer Church was founded by Pennsylvania Dutch using English for the first time in Milwaukee. *St. Johannes* (St. John's) Lutheran Church and School was built in 1872. Throughout the 19th and even part of the 20th centuries, many early Catholic and Lutheran churches conducted at least part of their services in German. In fact, St. Jacobi Evangelical Lutheran Church (1873) offered German services until 1971.

As for other religious groups, Emanu-El Synagogue was formed in 1849, while a German branch of the Methodist Episcopal Church was established on the west side of Milwaukee by 1850. Later, a German Baptist Congregation and a German Evangelical Church were established in Milwaukee.

Moreover, a Free Thinkers chapel in Painesville, now Franklin, a neighboring suburb south of Milwaukee, is being maintained by preservation-minded volunteers. In its yard is the only cemetery exclusively for Free Thinkers in the nation.

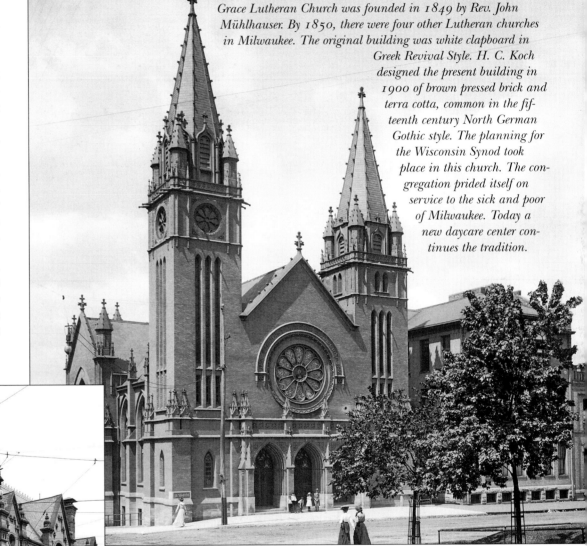

Grace Lutheran Church was founded in 1849 by Rev. John Mühlhauser. By 1850, there were four other Lutheran churches in Milwaukee. The original building was white clapboard in Greek Revival Style. H. C. Koch designed the present building in 1900 of brown pressed brick and terra cotta, common in the fifteenth century North German Gothic style. The planning for the Wisconsin Synod took place in this church. The congregation prided itself on service to the sick and poor of Milwaukee. Today a new daycare center continues the tradition.

In 1849, Emanu-El Synagogue (left) was formed. German Jews began arriving in 1844, and by 1856 there were a total of 200 families and three reformed congregations. Most spoke German, rather than Hebrew or Yiddish, and considered themselves first German, then Jewish.

St. Peter's Roman Catholic Church, Milwaukee's first Catholic church, moved from downtown to St. Francis Seminary Woods. Today it is part of Old World Wisconsin, an open-air history museum located in Eagle, Wisconsin, 35 miles southwest of Milwaukee.

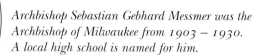

Archbishop Sebastian Gebhard Messmer was the Archbishop of Milwaukee from 1903 – 1930. A local high school is named for him.

St. Gall's Roman Catholic Church was built in 1849. The Jesuits made their first foothold in Milwaukee in 1855, when they were placed in charge of St. Gall's Church, North 3rd Street and Michigan Street (near the Milwaukee Road Depot).

Shown is the St. John's Lutheran Church and School in 1872. Mr. Nietschke (marked with X) is the maternal grandfather of Mayors Carl and Frank Zeidler. In 1889, a new building of German Gothic Revival-influenced architecture was built to house one of the oldest Lutheran congregations in the city. In 1900, the membership peaked as probably the largest Lutheran Church in the Midwest.

Gute Nacht......

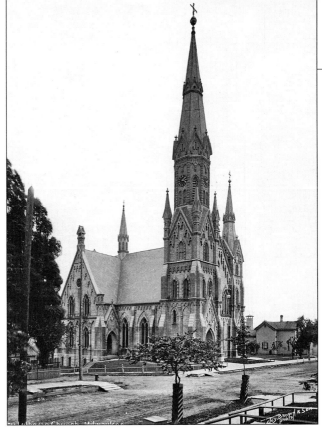

At the Sherman Park Lutheran Church, at Sherman Boulevard and Center Street, services in German are held occasionally.

Trinity Evangelical Lutheran Church, located at 9th and Highland Streets, built in 1847, became the mother church of the Missouri Synod. John Pritzlaff bought the land and donated it for the church to be built there. Concordia College was established through this church.

Holy Hill in Hartford, Wisconsin (30 miles north of Milwaukee), offers a spectacular view of the surrounding Kettle Moraine area. Holy Hill, National Shrine of Mary, Help of Christians was built in 1906 by a Roman Catholic Religious Order, now the Discalced Carmelites, at the request of Milwaukee Archbishop Sebastian Gebhard Messmer. It was granted the status of Minor Basilica by Pope Benedict XVI in 2006.

..... *Good Night*

This is the Certificate of Confirmation for 14-year-old Edward Brumder. He was confirmed at Grace Lutheran Church in Milwaukee on May 8, 1921.

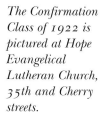

The Confirmation Class of 1922 is pictured at Hope Evangelical Lutheran Church, 35th and Cherry streets.

Many people attended the funeral for the Reverend Joseph H. Holzbauer at St. Joseph's Catholic Church.

As the city expanded, each neighborhood added a church or two for the convenience of the parishioners. Although many buildings have become houses of worship for other religions, the *Kirche* (church) inscription over the entrances remains. The churches gave spiritual sustenance to their parishioners in varied ways, including baptism, First Holy Communion, confirmation, wedding, funeral, and holiday celebrations.

The 1929 wedding picture of William and Augusta Hummel, who later became managers of the Freie Gemeinde *(Free Thinkers) at Jefferson Hall, the meeting place and activity center for Germans of the area.*

Gerda Dreher's First Holy Communion was held at St. Joseph's Catholic Church in 1937. Age seven was the usual age for this very special day.

Sherman Park Lutheran Church (left photo), along with other Milwaukee area churches, offers a German-language concert and service during the holidays. At Christmas time, the church is decorated with poinsettias and a nativity scene. Grace Lutheran Church (right photo) is also decorated for the holidays with Christmas trees.

CEMETERIES

Pabst Memorial

In Milwaukee's non-denominational Forest Home Cemetery visitors can recognize locally prominent names. Among these, buried in an area known as "Beer Baron's Corner," are the Pabst, Blatz, and Schlitz families. Nineteenth-century cemeteries were often regarded as parks, where families could picnic and spend the day with their loved ones. Calvary Cemetery for Catholics has a splendid and unique Gatehouse. In medieval times, for nobility, the eulogy was read at the gate of the cemetery. Union Cemetery is the earliest set aside for Lutherans. Both Union (on Teutonia Avenue) and Calvary are now closed to new burials. Methodists and Baptists had their cemeteries as well. Moreover, many burials took place on farms, in church yards, or in small cemeteries scattered in the area.

Blatz Mausoleum

Calvary Cemetery Gatehouse

The Schlitz Monument (left) has a carving of the S.S. Schiller, that sank off Land's End, England, and took the life of Joseph Schlitz.

MILWAUKEE: THE BEER CAPITAL

Prosit (cheers) was – and still is – a popular toast with a glass of beer for Germans and non-Germans alike. Early on, Germans preferred beer to the Yankees' whiskey, and it remains the beverage of choice for many today. Almost every street in the German neighborhood had a public saloon. Each was a social center with a *Stammtisch*, a table where the regulars gathered to discuss the day's events over a glass of beer. The discussions could be lively because immigrants came from various German-speaking provincial realms with rulers who had different points of view. In addition, a free lunchtime buffet of cold cuts and cheeses attracted business to these saloons.

In the 1880s, Third Street served as the main German shopping area in Milwaukee. Some shopkeepers even went so far as to place signs in the windows, which proclaimed "English Spoken Here" to attract non-German business. Of the many who made beer in their basements and served meals cooked by the women in the house, a few became large entrepreneurs.

The 1840s saw the beginning of the beer industry in Milwaukee. By 1849 Wisconsin had 22 breweries and 166 more were added in the next ten years. German immigrants provided brewing experience and were ready consumers. Yeast, malted barley, hops, and an ample supply of pure Wisconsin water contributed the formula basics for Milwaukee's popular product. Milwaukee's location on Lake Michigan granted a means of transportation, and logging in Wisconsin's Northwoods provided the wood for barrels. Milwaukee area farmers supplied the required hops and barley, while Milwaukee's cold weather produced ice for lager beer production. Indeed, lager needs temperatures under 40 degrees so the yeast can ferment at the bottom of the barrel. Milwaukee has high bluffs surrounding its marshland where storage caves for beer were located. Milwaukee was the perfect place to brew beer.

As early as 1841, Hermann Reutelshöfer established the first German brewery in Walker's Point. It changed owners, first Meyer, then Neukirch, who partnered with Charles T. Melms in 1848. By 1856 the city had two dozen breweries. When Melms alone took over in 1859, he converted the brewery grounds into a beer garden, probably the first of many.

In 1842, Jacob Best, Sr., began his brewery. His four sons worked all aspects of their small operation. Jacob retired in 1860, at which time, his son, Phillip, took control. Soon after, Phillip's daughter, Marie, married Captain Frederick

While today we have the "Coffee Break," Milwaukeeans of yesteryear enjoyed a "Beer Break." This Kesseljunge *(beer bucket boy) carried ten buckets, sometimes 12, to deliver beer to factory and office workers. He was expected to be punctual. Often he delivered to a business twice each day, once at 9:30 am and again at 3:00 pm.*

The workers were glad to see the smiling beer delivery fellow as he carefully balanced beer buckets for them.

Pabst, who then went into the brewing business with his father-in-law. In 1869, they bought Melm's and it became the South Side Brewery. At the national convention of brewers in St. Louis in 1876, Best was named the best beer in the country. Someone tied blue ribbons around the necks of the bottles and people subsequently asked for the "Blue Ribbon Beer." It was this brew that would eventually become known as "Pabst Blue Ribbon Beer."

Hops for the brew was grown at the Captain's Farm, in what is now Washington Heights Subdivision. Phillip bought out his brothers and retired in 1866. When he died in 1869, Emil Schandein and Fred Pabst took over and ran the Best Brewery. Then in 1889 the name was changed to The Pabst Brewing Company. At that time it was the largest brewery in the world. "He drinks BEST who drinks PABST." Ironically, only in that year – 1889 – was beer the number one industry in Milwaukee.

Along with Pabst, other Milwaukee brewers, including Blatz, Miller, and Schlitz, grew to national importance. As such, the "ideal city" ultimately produced a barrel of beer a year for every man, woman, and child in America.

Miller and Pawlett started an ale brewery in 1843, and when Levi Blossom took over, it became the Eagle Brewery.

In 1846, John Braun began the City Brewery and in 1851, Valentin Blatz, a Bavarian-trained brewmaster, built a brewery next door. The breweries were combined and after Braun died, Blatz married his widow. In 1875, Blatz became the first Milwaukee brewer to bottle beer. The brewer did so at a rate of 2,000 bottles per day. By 1884, Blatz was the third largest brewery in Milwaukee, the first to distribute nationally and the first to use mechanical refrigeration, manufactured in Milwaukee by the Vilter Company. Pabst Brewing purchased The Blatz Brewery in 1950. By 1959 Blatz had ceased operation. It was the first of the "Big Four" to close. The main office became the Beer Baron's Restaurant for a time. Along with the bottling house, it later became part of Milwaukee School of Engineering (MSOE). Another plant building houses apartment condominiums.

August Krug founded his brewery in 1849. His bookkeeper, Joseph Schlitz, bought the business when Krug died in 1856. Schlitz then married Krug's widow and the name was changed to Jos. Schlitz Brewing Co. in 1870. The Great Chicago Fire of 1871 saw Schlitz sending shipments of beer by rail – a new aspect of the business was begun. At the time of his death in 1875, four of the Uihlein brothers were working there and eventually took controlling ownership. But the Schlitz name remained. Its slogan, "Schlitz – the Beer that made Milwaukee Famous," has endured.

The Gipfel Brewery, erected in 1853 on West Juneau Avenue by David Gipfel, is the oldest remaining brewery building in the city. His sons ran the busi-

Beer was stored in barrels; coopers were needed to make and repair the barrels. These coopers are pictured not only with barrels, but also with a Schnitzelbank *(a carving bench). The* Schnitzelbank *is a popular German icon which sparked numerous skits, plays, and songs—some of which are performed even today.*

ness until 1892. Their specialty in 1872 was *Weiss Bier* (wheat beer).

In 1856 Strohn & Reitzenstein started to build a brewery but they died of cholera. George Schweickart bought the assets and built the Menomonee Brewery. He sold it to his son-in-law, Adam Gettelman, whose family continued the business until they sold to Miller in 1961.

Also in 1856, Bavarian immigrant Franz Falk opened a brewery which became the fourth largest, trailing behind Pabst, Schlitz and Blatz. In time it became Falk, Jung & Borchert Brewery. After two fires, they sold out to Pabst in 1892. Herman Falk opened a machine shop, then a foundry, which

became a producer of giant precision industrial gears. Today, it is called the Falk Corporation.

Jacob Best's son, Charles, started the Plank Road Brewery in 1848. His brother and partners died, so in 1855, Charles sold to Frederick Miller, an experienced brewmaster from Siegmaringen, Germany, for $9,000 in gold. The name was changed to Menomonee Valley Brewery. The brewhouse was built in 1886 but was destroyed by fire in 1891. Then, the famous Miller Beer Garden, the site of many weekend festivities, was built on the hill. In 1970, Philip Morris purchased Miller. At the time of sale Miller employed 2,300 people. Today, Miller is the second largest brewery in

the U.S. It has contracts to produce Pabst and Schlitz beers; has branches in 80 countries and was sold to South African Breweries for $5.6 billion in 2002. Over the years the Miller family has contributed greatly to the Milwaukee community, as exemplified by the efforts of Fred Miller, who in the 1950s ensured that his hometown had a major league baseball team and a world class theatre.

Beer has so pervaded the culture of Milwaukee that a railroad line famous for transporting beer received the nickname, "the Beer line," and through the mid-twentieth century, rarely did a get-together not include the singing of *Im Himmel Gibt's Kein Bier* (In Heaven There Ain't No Beer).

Beer wagons were a common sight on Milwaukee streets. They went from saloon to saloon, wagons piled high with beer barrels for delivery. At each stop, the customers were so happy to see them that they invited the drivers to join them for a drink.

Here a Schlitz horse-drawn wagon delivers cases of bottled beer.

Eventually beer companies made the switch from horses to motorized vehicles to distribute their product. A proud deliveryman sits at the front of a Pabst truck on his way to delivering many barrels of Milwaukee's Blue Ribbon Beer. Like most breweries, Pabst eventually sold beer in bottles.

GETTELMAN

Peter and Katherine Gettelman brought their two children from Darmstadt, Germany to Germantown, Wisconsin in Washington County, (16 miles northwest of Milwaukee). Their son, Adam, not wanting to become a farmer, went to brewing school in Milwaukee, where he apprenticed at the Menomonee Brewery founded by George Schweickhart.

Adam married Magdalena, the boss' daughter, in 1870. A year later, he had a financial interest in the brewery, and by 1876 he owned it outright. The name changed to A. Gettelman Brewing Co. in 1887. He and Magdalena's two sons, William and Frederick, eventually took over the brewery. Ultimately, William went into banking at the West Side Bank, while Frederick, known as Fritz, ran the brewing operation. He originally wanted to be an engineer, but was successful running the family company, where he improved brewing practice and equipment. The company trademark "Fritzie," and the slogan "Get, Get, Get Gettelman," both attributed to him, can be found in faded paint on walls around town. Fritz also invented the six-pack of non-returnable bottles in 1949 and called it a "Basket O' Beer." Gettelman's slogan, "The Beer Without a Peer," ran as print ads.

Miller and Gettelman Breweries were across the street from each other. Together they paid the city to extend a water line into the valley, which at that time was outside the city limits. This insured a reliable source of water for their beer formulas. In 1961 Gettleman sold out to Miller.

In 1891 Adam Gettelman advertised an offer of $1,000 to anyone able to prove that their premium beer was brewed with anything other than pure malt, hops, and water. No one ever collected.

MILLER

Frederic J. Miller was born into a prosperous middle class merchant family in Riedlingen, Württemberg in 1824. His father had been a man of large means but lost most of his fortune by speculation in coffee, tea, and woolen goods during the Napoleonic wars. At age 14, Frederic went to France where he studied for seven years. He also traveled in Europe and Africa. He studied with his uncle, a brewer, and eventually bought the lease of the Royal Brewery at Siegmaringen, Hohenzollern. He sold it in 1854 to sail to America.

The family traveled leisurely by lake and river steamers and decided to settle in Wisconsin, a land very much like their home. Frederic purchased the Plank Road Brewery from Charles Best for cash in 1855 and brewed 300 barrels of beer, made from local hops and barley, and yeast which he had hand-carried from Germany. Sadly, his wife and four of their five children died in a cholera epidemic in Milwaukee, and in 1860 he married Lisette Gross, a local girl from Hales Corners, a southwestern suburb. They had five children, three boys and two girls.

Daughter Clara married Carl A. Miller from Württemberg, Germany. This new immigrant had an entrepreneurial spirit and bought Wisconsin forestland. His last retail outlet was the Carl Miller Lumber Company in Milwaukee. Then, in 1888, the founder of the brewery, Frederic J. Miller, died at the age of sixty-three. Four of his and Lisette's five children became president of the brewery at various times. Although only Frederic J. Miller's daughters had children, the Miller name was carried on because of the son-in-law, Carl A. Miller.

Frederic J. Miller purchased the bankrupt Plank Road Brewery from Charles Best in 1855, and renamed it the Menomonee Valley Brewery. When Miller died in 1888, the name was changed to Miller Brewing Company.

Miller Inn began as a neighborhood tavern and is a landmark. It is visible on the hill in Miller Valley. Workers climbed farther up the hill to the family house where they ate four times each day.

This 1892 picture shows the size of the Miller complex, which covered the valley.

The Miller Girls dressed in high boots and festive costumes to advertise that Miller excelled in "High Life." They toast "the Champagne of Bottled Beer."

This winter scene of Miller Valley, looking north across the Menomonee marshes, shows the ice used in the brewing and storage processes.

In 1903 Miller High Life was introduced in slender, clear bottles. During Prohibition Miller made health drinks, malt syrup, and soft drinks. In 1938 they trademarked the famous "Girl in the Moon."

Energetic grandson Frederick C. Miller graduated from the University of Notre Dame in 1929 and went into his father's lumber business. In 1947 he became president of the brewery. His Clara Miller family branch owned only 3% of the stock, but that 3% was the deciding vote between his two cousins in 1946 for control of the brewery. In 1953, Fred brought Major League Baseball to Milwaukee and the Milwaukee Braves played at County Stadium. They won the pennant in 1957 by beating the Yankees.

The Miller name still supports Milwaukee major league baseball to this day, as the recently built stadium is called Miller Park.

In December 1954, Fred Miller, returning from a Notre Dame football game, landed at the Milwaukee airport. He and his son Fred were to continue on their hunting and fishing vacation to Canada, but crashed while taking off from Mitchell Field. They both died.

Miller bought Gettleman, their neighbor across the street in the Menomonee Valley in 1961. Then, in 1966, control of the Miller Brewery went out of the family. Lorraine John Mulberger, the immigrant Fred's granddaughter, sold her 52% for $39 million to W. R. Grace & Co. Three years later, in 1969, W.R.

Grace sold those shares to Phillip Morris for $130 million. At that time, her brother, Harry John, Jr., sold his minority share to Philip Morris for $97 million (she should have waited!) His money was added to his De Rance Foundation, a non-profit Catholic charity he had begun in 1947. It grew to become the largest Catholic charity in the world. Today it has virtually vanished due to mismanagement.

In 1975, Miller was the number four brewer in the nation. In that same year, Miller introduced Miller Lite Beer internationally. Two years later, Miller was ranked number two after Budweiser, a rank it still holds. Today, Miller is owned by South African Breweries and its stock is listed on the London Stock Exchange.

The Cave Museum at Miller Brewery reminds everyone that before mechanical refrigeration, beer was kept ice-cold in Milwaukee area caves.

This was the first in the popular series of the "Girl in the Moon" Miller Brewery advertising campaign. Miller family legend claims the model was either Mrs. Carl Miller or one of her daughters.

PABST

Frederick C. Pabst came to America in 1848 and settled in Chicago with his parents. His mother and siblings died in a cholera epidemic there. He worked as a waiter for $5 a month, but at fourteen he signed on to a Goodrich Line steamer as a cabin boy. He worked his way up by studying navigation and received a steamboat pilot's certificate in 1857 when he was 21 years old. Eventually he became part owner and captain of the *Huron*, the first boat of the Goodrich Great Lakes fleet. Chicago District Inspectors licensed him as a "first class pilot" for Lake Michigan, which qualified him to navigate all classes of vessels. In an 1863 storm, he was forced to run his steamer *Seabird* ashore off Whitefish Bay, a village north of Milwaukee.

In 1862, he married Marie Best, and two years later he bought a partnership in the Jacob Best Brewing Company from Marie's grandfather, Jacob Best, who then retired. The Pabsts had eleven children, of whom five survived.

The Captain bought Falk, Jung, & Borchert Brewery whose operations had been disrupted by fires in 1889 and 1892. There was a family connection because Phillip Jung (from the Jung Brewery) had married Jacob Best Jr.'s daughter, Dora.

A lager, bottled under the name Best Select, was a popular beer which the Phillip

Emil Schandein

Jacob Best

Best Brewing Company entered in competitions, gaining several awards and often winning against its rival Budweiser. In 1882, the company started selling the Select with a blue ribbon tied around the neck to signify it was an award-winning beer, a practice that lasted until 1916. Many people also chose what was to become known as Pabst Blue Ribbon due to its labeling as "union made beer."

Phillip Best's sons-in-law, Emil Schandein and the Captain, built the brewery into the nation's largest from 1895-1902. The Captain traveled throughout the world selling Pabst Beer.

In 1889, after Emil Schandein's death, the company name became The Pabst Brewing Company. Pabst owned real estate all around the country, including a saloon located at Times Square, Manhattan, where New Year's Eve is celebrated every year. His building came down when the Broadway subway was tunneled beneath it.

The Captain was a generous contributor to the cultural and social life of Milwaukee. He built the Pabst Theater, was an investor in the Kirby-St. Charles Hotel and the Pabst Building which housed his First National Bank. He developed the *Schützen Park* (Sharpshooters Park) and the Whitefish Bay Park (five miles

View of the Pabst compound (originally the Best Empire Brewery) on the hill on Chestnut Street (now Juneau).

north of downtown), which Milwaukeeans visited via excursion boat from downtown. They enjoyed summer afternoons drinking Pabst Blue Ribbon Beer on the Whitefish Bay bluff where the *Seabird* met its demise.

On hilly ground, just west of Milwaukee, the Pabst farm grew hops for the brewery and raised Percheron horses. The Captain had his summer home there. In 1892, with his backing, a streetcar line went into service along Pabst Avenue (now Lloyd Street) between Wauwatosa and Milwaukee. The presence of the streetcar line made the development of the neighborhood inevitable. After the Captain died in 1904, the Pabst family built a high-end subdivision there called The Highlands.

Captain Frederick Pabst

Elder son, Gustav, married Hilda Lemp of the St. Louis brewing family. Gustav also ran the Pabst Brewery. The Captain's other son, Fred, Jr., married Ida Uihlein, first daughter of August Uihlein of the Schlitz Brewery.

In 1906, the Pabst Brewing Company began using caps on bottles instead of corks. Pabst was the second brewer to put beer in cans in 1935. Called "Export," they came with a picture of a can opener on the side, with instructions on how to open the can.

During Prohibition, Fred took over Gustav's shares in the Pabst Brewery and took over the management. Barely surviving the impact of the 18th Amendment, Pabst produced near beer, malt extracts, syrups, and processed cheese until it was repealed in 1933. Gustav kept the real estate in the bargain. He owned hundreds of acres of land in Waukesha's "Lake Country" (35 miles west of

Milwaukee) where he built a 28,000 square foot hunting lodge in the style of European royalty. Titled Hungarian princes and others of similar background visited and hunted there. However, he was forced to sell or develop most of the land during the Depression.

Over the years, Frederick and Ida Pabst acquired nearly 2,000 acres near Oconomowoc (35 miles west of Milwaukee). They raised crops for the local cannery as well as prized Percherons and pedigreed Holstein cattle. Today that land is known as Pabst Farms with a master plan for a community on 1,500 acres.

In 1943, Pabst started advertising on national radio networks, but it was not until 1950 when Pabst sponsored boxing on CBS TV that production and sales began to soar. With Pabst Brewing Company growing, Fred Pabst retired as chairman of the board in May 1954.

Pabst was purchased in a leveraged buyout by Mill Valley, California-based S & P Co., founded by Paul Kalmanovitz, in 1985, at which time corporate headquarters were moved from Milwaukee to San Antonio, Texas. In 1996, Pabst closed its Milwaukee Brewery. However, in 1999, Pabst bought Strohs Brewing Company, including its interest in previously Heilman-owned product names such as Old Style. Shortly thereafter, Pabst licensed the brewing rights of all Pabst-owned products to Miller. Finally, the Kalmanovitz Charitable Trust was granted ownership of Pabst in 2000. Due to Federal Tax Laws, the Trust divested itself of the brewery stock in 2005.

As such, in recent years Pabst has now

become a "virtual brewer" in that it retains ownership of the Pabst Blue Ribbon brand, its flagship beer, and 28 other brands. Miller, by contract, brews each one. Pabst brands today include PBR, Old Milwaukee, Old Style, Lone Star, Schlitz, McSorley's, Olympia, Strohs, and Colt 45.

Gustav Pabst

Fred Pabst Jr.

Horse-drawn wagons delivered beer barrels to customers. Each barrel contained 31 gallons of beer. The drivers were paid $3 a day.

Milwaukee, Wis.
The Pabst Building. — Das Pabst-Gebäude.

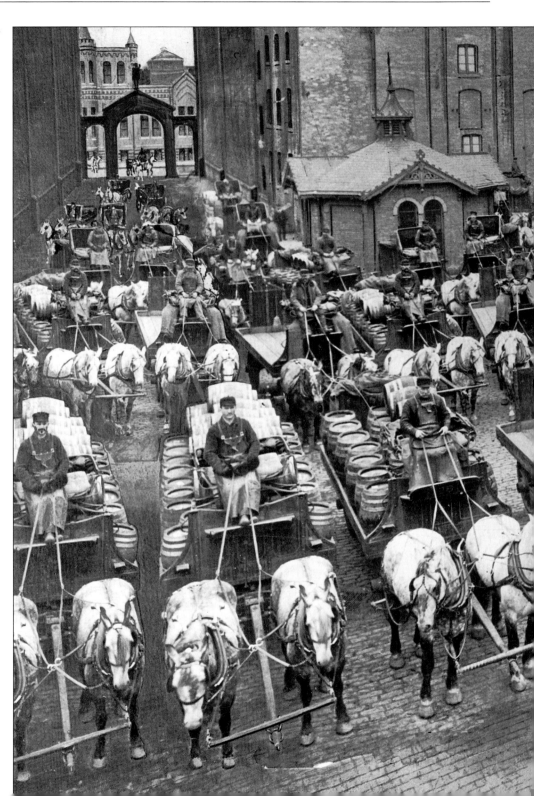

The Pabst Building was built on the site of Solomon Juneau's trading post in 1891. It was 235 feet high and included a tower with a clock. Many couples took the elevator to the tower, climbed 75 steps and were married at the top. It was demolished and replaced by the present 110 East Building. The arched entrance could not be saved so it was replicated.

PABST BREWING CO'S BOTTLED BEER and TONIC.

BLATZ

Johann Valentin "Val" Blatz was born in 1825 at Miltenberg on the Main River in Bavaria. At the age of 14 he entered his father's brewery as an apprentice. At 18, he traveled in Germany, visiting and working in various breweries, gaining experience, and in 1848, immigrated to America. He stopped in Buffalo for a year and settled in Milwaukee in 1849, establishing a brewery next door to John Braun's City Brewery. Shortly after, he became brewmaster there. When Braun died in 1852, Valentin merged the breweries and married the widow, Luise. The combined breweries produced 350 barrels that year. By 1880 they produced 125,000 barrels, and in 1884, they were the third largest brewery in Milwaukee.

Blatz had many "firsts." They were first to distribute nationally with distribution centers in Chicago, New York, Boston, New Orleans, Memphis, and Savannah; first to bottle beer; first to use mechanical refrigeration which was manufactured by the Vilter Company of Milwaukee.

A fire in 1872 destroyed the brewery buildings, but he rebuilt larger, covering more than four city blocks. Blatz beer was awarded the highest premium given at the Centennial Exposition at Philadelphia and the Cotton Exposition of New Orleans in 1885. In 1890 he sold out to a group of London investors who owned the brewery until Prohibition. Valentin Blatz died in St. Paul, Minnesota, on the job, promoting Blatz beer.

After producing more than a million barrels a year in the 1940s and '50s, Blatz sold out to Pabst in 1958. Today, the buildings have been converted into residential condominiums and office space. The former headquarters with the Blatz trademark on the pediment is now the Milwaukee School of Engineering (MSOE) Alumni Center, and the former bottling plant for Blatz, then for Pabst, is now the MSOE Student Center.

Johann Valentin "Val" Blatz

Val's son, Albert and Adam Gettelman, two of Milwaukee's most prominent brewers, spare a moment for a photo on the Blatz Farm.

SCHLITZ

In 1849, August Krug from Miltenberg, Germany started a small restaurant in Milwaukee and produced 250 barrels of beer in the basement. His wife, Anna, waited on tables. His sister, Katherine and her husband Benedikt Uihlein lived in Bavaria and owned *"Zur Krone"* (the Crown), a *Gasthaus* (inn). Their eldest son, eight-year-old August Uihlein, came to America with his grandfather Krug. Their ship caught fire and by holding on to a floating wooden box they survived until rescued by the sailors on the American *S.S. Devonshire.*

The old man brought $800 in gold coin to Milwaukee for his son Krug, August Uihlein's namesake. Krug spent the windfall to hire helpers. One was

Joseph Schlitz was also vice president of the Second Ward Savings Bank, one of the founders of the Brewers' Fire Insurance Company of America, secretary of the Milwaukee Brewers' Association, a Mason and a member of the West Side Turnverein (1857) and numerous other societies.

Joseph Schlitz, who had learned bookkeeping in his native Mainz and had worked for a large firm in Frankfurt. After Krug's death at age 40, his widow, Anna, married Joseph Schlitz. She never had any children.

Joseph Schlitz, at the age of 25, took over the management of the brewery, in the interests of Mrs. Krug, wisely investing his savings in the business to become the widow's partner. They married two years later and changed the name of the brewery

The Uihlein Brothers owned and operated the Schlitz Brewery. They were born in Wertheim, Bavaria to Benedikt Uihlein and Katherine Krug Uihlein. All eventually came to Milwaukee. August, Henry, Edward and Alfred were the majority owners.

to his own, the Jos. Schlitz Brewing Company. In 1858, the storage capacity increased to 2,000 barrels.

August Uihlein went to school in Milwaukee and St. Louis. He entered the brewing business in St. Louis before he returned to Milwaukee. His Uihlein brothers, as adults, eventually meandered to Milwaukee to work at the brewery.

Between 1870 and 1871, Joseph Schlitz erected the greater part of the brewery, which remains today at the corner of 3rd and Walnut streets.

After the 1871 Chicago fire, Schlitz shipped beer as a substitute for the shortage of water there, which was a well-received gesture. Brewery sales doubled the next year. "The Beer That Made Milwaukee Famous" became the trademark slogan.

Brothers August, Henry, Edward, and Alfred Uihlein all worked at the brewery when Joseph Schlitz set sail for Germany in 1875. The steamship *S.S. Schiller* sank in a storm. All aboard were lost. The tragedy shocked all of Milwaukee.

Joseph Schlitz was buried in Forest Home Cemetery in an area known as "Beer Barons' Corner," facing the memorials of brewers Blatz and Pabst.

After Joseph's death, control of the company was turned over to the Uihlein brothers. When Anna Schlitz died in 1887, most of the rest of the stock was purchased by the Uihleins from her beneficiaries.

In 1879, Schlitz bought Quentin Park, and quickly reopened it, complete with a theater, zoo, and fountains. As Schlitz Park, it accommodated up to 20,000 patrons. It is known as Carver Park today. They also operated the Schlitz Hotel with its very popular Palm Garden Restaurant.

Schlitz Brewing was the first to brew beer from a pure yeast culture, brought from Denmark in 1885 by brother William Uihlein.

In 1886, the company had 12 ice houses on the Milwaukee River north of the city and harvested 100,000 tons of ice. Half of the ice was used for shipment by rail car and half

for cooling the beer in the caves.

By 1911, Schlitz introduced the brown glass bottle which became famous because it insured the stability and quality of the beer.

After Prohibition, Erwin Uihlein, youngest son of August, ran Schlitz with the help of Sol Abrams, general manager. In 1961, Robert A. Uihlein, Jr. took charge. In 1969, Schlitz was the first American brewer to enter the European market. Two years later the brewery began manufacturing its own aluminum cans.

By that time the Schlitz complex had grown from national to international distribution. In response, Schlitz not only built

new plants to be more efficient regionally, but also quickened the beer making process, a decision which resulted in a consequent loss of quality. Thus, consumer ventures in Asia and elsewhere failed.

The Brewery Workers Union pressured management in 1978 to meet recent contract terms with Miller and Pabst. The Milwaukee plant closed soon after, and in the summer of 1982, Strohs Brewery in Michigan bought the business for about five cents on the dollar.

Some other related Schlitz small ventures were corner saloons, the Schlitz Hotel and Palm Garden, E-Line Chocolate Company and the Schlitz Circus Parade.

The brewery began sponsoring the Schlitz Circus Parade in 1963. Every year, in the middle of July, authentic antique wagons from several circuses paraded through downtown Milwaukee. Cheering crowds saw clowns, marching bands, celebrities, wild animals, costumed ladies riding their horses, and a 40-horse hitch.

Schlitz: "THE BEER THAT MADE MILWAUKEE FAMOUS" was known the world over.

PROHIBITION IN MILWAUKEE

In 1920, the Anti-Saloon League and Women's Christian Temperance Union achieved success in their efforts "to save the individuals who drank too much." Thus, National Prohibition became the law of the land. Its effect proved to be severely damaging to some brewing companies and completely catastrophic to others. In Milwaukee, beer production at over 25 breweries ended. Employees dwindled from 3,217 in l910 to 512 in 1920. As many breweries closed, so did a good number of ancillary businesses. Indeed, manufacturers of barrels, yeast, boxes, glassware, bar fixtures, etc. were forced to cease production.

However, the larger brewers diversified and produced near beer, as well as malt syrup and malt tonic. Pabst added cheese products, while Blatz and Miller bottled soda and water. Many of the Schlitz heirs invested in the E-Line Chocolate Company. They built fancy red-brick buildings north on the Milwaukee River, with a fireplace in each office. Then they set about making chocolate, but, unfortunately, never perfected the formula. The chocolate would turn white and melt in the heat. Not surprisingly, the enterprise failed.

Despite the federal law, the desire for beer and liquor did not end. Illegal imports came from Canada. Doctors prescribed whiskey as the only cure for the flu and wrote prescriptions for "medicinal spirits." Amateur chemists made wine and distilled schnapps. *Heimgemacht* (home brew), as the Germans called it, became all the rage. This verse was a popular ditty about home brew:

> *Mother's in the kitchen, washing out the jugs;*
> *Sister's in the pantry, bottling the suds;*
> *Father's in the cellar, mixing up the hops;*
> *Johnny's on the porch, watching for the cops.*

Ingredients for beer and liquor were in high demand because consumers made it for home consumption. The Milwaukee Public Library could not fulfill all the requests for books on do-it-yourself brewing.

Milwaukeeans joyfully sang "Happy Days Are Here Again," when Congress repealed the Amendment in April 1933. A *Volksfest* at the Milwaukee Auditorium heralded the good news, and the Germans were in full swing with their singing and yodeling, bratwurst and sauerkraut – some even stood in line the night before Prohibition was repealed to be the first to get a taste of "legal beer."

Six breweries re-emerged following Prohibition. Blatz, Braumeister, Gettelman, Miller, Pabst, and Schlitz continued producing beer into mid-century. So busy was the industry that brewery-related railroad traffic made up over half of the rail business.

Schlitz's first bottling works in 1877 put up over 1,000,000 bottles of beer and that number steadily increased, necessitating new quarters north of downtown on 3rd Street. The effect of Prohibition on Schlitz was staggering. But it recovered, and in 1952, Schlitz set a record as the first brewery ever to produce 6,000,000 barrels of beer in one year.

GERMAN INDUSTRY

While beer is the first product people think of as being "Milwaukee," in only one year (1890) was beer the number one industry in the city. Beer and its predominant impression eclipsed numerous other industries without which the community of Milwaukee could not have survived. Lumber for housing; grist mills for food; hides for tanning; room and board facilities for workers; churches; livery stables and blacksmiths – all were necessities which the Germans provided.

As a group, the majority of Germans were literate. Therefore, they demanded print material. Publishers provided books, magazines, newspapers, broadsides, bulletins, etc. German know-how and skill provided the invention of new machinery for these enterprises, which then laid the foundation for mechanization and the next phase in the industrial revolution. Production of machinery became a major industry and was a transition from small workshops to large factories and offices. By 1900, metal fabrication was the local leading industry.

In 1859 there were 558 manufacturers in Milwaukee County. By 1866, the Milwaukee Iron Company produced rails for the railroads, while Toepfer Iron Works made castings and bent sheet metal. These and other iron manufacturers helped to change the economy from commerce to manufacturing. The nickname "Machine Shop of the World" was well-earned at the time as workers believed in quality and took pride in their work, characteristics attributed to their training and (German) upbringing. By 1900, the total production of all machine shops and foundries' net earnings in Milwaukee equaled 15 million dollars.

Notable Milwaukee businesses over the years have included Kleinsteuber's Machine Shop on State Street where Latham Sholes invented the first practical typewriter in 1867. Geuder, Paeschke & Frey made tin utensils and baking ware starting in 1880; Kieckhefer's National Enameling and Stamping Company initials spell out NESCO – yes, the well-known roaster!

Many farmers throughout the Midwest grew wheat because it was a profitable crop to grow in the previously undeveloped land. By 1848, warehouse capacity was one million bushels. Five flour mills were in operation with a combined manufacturing output of 500 barrels per day. In 1862, Milwaukee was one of the primary wheat markets in the world. By 1870, the grains traded included flaxseed, hay, flour, and feeds. However, during these years there were also numerous economic downturns due to the overproduction of wheat. Early farmers did not employ crop rotation, thereby depleting the soil. Dairy products emerged as the most viable alternative to wheat, and by 1899, more than 90% of Wisconsin farms kept cows. As of 1915 Wisconsin produced more cheese annually than any other state.

TANNING AND LEATHER

Tanning was one of early Milwaukee's big three major industries, providing employment for many – especially Germans who knew the trade from "home" and were industrious workers. Tanning became "a distinctly German stronghold."

Tanneries were situated on the Milwaukee and Menomonee Rivers for ready access to the most important ingredient in the tanning process: water, needed for washing and rinsing the hides. These rivers also afforded ready access for transporting product. What's more, nearby tamarack trees, when processed, provided the necessary tannin.

Farmers brought the stock to the slaughter houses; meat packers, in turn, took the hides to the tanners. After the tanning, the finished skins went to the factories where leather goods such as shoes, gloves, belts for people and machinery, workers' aprons, saddles, halters, harnesses, and other leather items were made. Army boots and cartridge belts for the Civil War soldiers were also manufactured. The growth from 13 tanneries in 1860, to 30 tanning businesses in 1872, illustrates just how huge the industry was. By 1890 Milwaukee was the largest producer of plain, tanned leather in the world.

Calf hides are being processed at the Gallun Tannery.

August Gallun

Albert Trostel

Trostel and Gallun, originally partners, built separate tanneries on the Milwaukee River. Trostel featured side leather for shoes; Gallun, fine calf leather.

Finished hides became shoes, gloves, harnesses, and belts to drive machines.

Fred Vogel

Guido Pfister

The Pfister and Vogel leather company was one of the largest tanneries in America in the early 20th century. It provided shoe leather for soldiers during the First World War. Other tanners included Zohrlaut; J. F. Schoellkopf; C. Anstedt; G. B. Vollhardt; and W. Gerhard Becher. Today some tanneries remain active including Seidel Tanning Corp.

39

This x-ray device checked the fit of shoes — children tried on "new" shoes and placed their feet in a box which showed their foot bones in the shoe. The x-ray was found to be seriously damaging and was later outlawed.

F. Mayer Boot and Shoe Manufacturing Company, established in 1877, eventually employed 1,600 workers. Their 1910 factory is now on the National Register of Historic Places. Their salesmen fanned out into the countryside, selling their wares to small town shoe stores. During WWI, they provided lunches and daycare for their employees' children. With the popularity of the automobile and consumers' changing tastes, people in the countryside drove to the big cities to purchase their shoes and ignored the small-town stores. These, along with the changing retail market, led to the company's demise in 1928.

Weyenberg Shoe Manufacturing Company (now WeyCo Group, Inc.) was known for its stylish shoes. It produced and distributed first-line shoes, among them Nunn-Bush and Florsheim. It also contributed to the development of the first shoe-fitting fluoroscope (top photo), which was built in Milwaukee in 1924.

In its heyday, the Milwaukee plant of Krause Milling Company ground three million pounds of corn every day. Its customers were breweries, foundries, and manufacturers of gypsum wall board. The plant was sold to Archer Daniels Midland in 1986 and demolished in 2006. Neighbors were Froedtert and Kurth Malting. Today the Milwaukee Journal Sentinel's new printing plant is located there.

Kurtis R. Froedtert had a life-long interest in medicine. He aspired to attend medical school, but his father died in 1915. Kurtis took over the family business, founded in 1869, and led it to become one of the largest malting concerns in the nation (shown below). Through his foresight and benevolence, he established the Froedtert Foundation for a "special" hospital— one which was different from others — which became the region's premier teaching hospital, the Medical College of Wisconsin.

Adolph C. ("AC") Zinn was born in 1849 to parents from Saxony, Germany. Schooled as a bookkeeper, he began the second malting business in the city in 1873. It eventually produced two million bushels of malted barley, thereby motivating local farmers to plant more of the crop. Barley became the largest crop in Wisconsin, which offset the declining wheat production. AC ultimately merged the malt business with Asmuth Malt and Grain. In fact, AC had a reputation for creating successful businesses, in that he became a director of the West Side Bank, a charter member and president of the Milwaukee Liederkranz and further, underwrote the Meadow Springs Distillery, which eventually became Red Star Yeast.

Adolph C. Zinn

Adolph Meinecke, born in Oldenburg, Germany, 1830, came to Milwaukee in 1854 and developed two successful business enterprises. His toy company and willow ware concern both employed many people. His toys were made of wood, while his furniture and baskets were all made of Wisconsin willow. The willow ware business also produced straw and artificial flowers. His basket business was the largest in the country at the time. He also supported the German-English Academy and its Engelmann Museum. His factory, built in 1891 on Wells Street, remains in use as an apartment building. One of Meinecke's factory buildings is pictured here.

The two largest clothing manufacturing companies in Milwaukee were the Friend Brothers Clothing Company, the largest, and the Adler Clothing Company, which grew to be one of the largest wholesale clothing houses in the United States. The Friend Brothers came from Bavaria where their father was a member of the Body Guard of the King, and fought under Napoleon against the Austrians. The brothers made men's clothing and invented a machine to cut multiple layers of cloth, which reduced hand work. This and these sewing machines sped up production. The oldest brother, Henry Friend, drowned on the same ship as Joseph Schlitz. The Friends and the Adler families intermarried. Prominent architect David Adler came from this family. Other notable Milwaukee clothing manufacturers included Eagle Knitting Company and the Phoenix Hosiery, founded in 1897, which made knit goods, such as gloves, scarves and mittens. Between 1910 and 1920, the business manufactured women's hosiery. In 1922, the name of the company was changed to the Phoenix Hosiery Company, which was sold in 1959.

The electrical industry ignited in Milwaukee with the help of graduates from School of Engineering of Milwaukee, where they learned about electrical technology. The photo shows one of the early classes at night in a boiler room.

Wehr Steel in West Allis (in Milwaukee County) was once the second largest steel foundry in the state of Wisconsin. Todd Wehr was the last surviving member of the Wehr Family. He set up a philanthropic foundation in 1953, which donated millions to educational projects in Wisconsin, among them the Todd Wehr Theater (Performing Arts in downtown Milwaukee), the Wehr Nature Center (in southern Milwaukee County), the Wehr Science Center, the Todd Wehr Theater (Marquette University), and the Todd Wehr Conference Center (Milwaukee School of Engineering). Prior to Wehr's death in 1965, Robert L. Manegold, whose family owned Dings Magnetic Separator, bought Wehr Steel. Interlocking Board and family relationships caused Robert L. Manegold to become president. In 1986, Wehr Steel was sold and the name changed.

In 1871, Biersach & Niedermeyer formed a partnership in Milwaukee. They located their tin shop in a small room on Market Square. They outgrew those quarters and moved several times while manufacturing ornamental iron, tin roofs, gutters, and downspouts, as well as other metal fabrication. During the First World War, women employees manufactured ammunition chests and machine gun stands. Before closing the business in the late 1980s, they made grills for Excalibur cars and air raid warning sirens. At their plant in Columbus, Wisconsin (80 miles northwest of Milwaukee), they made outdoor electrical enclosures.

Bavarian immigrant Franz Falk opened his first brewery in 1856. A later partnership with Frederick Goes resulted in the Bavaria Brewery. Falk joined with Jung and Borchert in 1889, but, unfortunately, a fire in 1892 destroyed all the major buildings and the partnership sold all their remaining interests to Pabst. However, even after the sale, the Falk name would go on in business. Herman Falk, the sixth child of Franz Falk and Louisa Wahl Falk (sister of Christian Wahl, the father of the Milwaukee Park system), opened a machine shop and foundry which produced precision industrial gears. In the mid-1930s, Falk forgave all employee debts accumulated during the Depression. The Falk Corporation created massive gears for the Navy in WWII. In addition, after retiring as a Brigadier General of the Wisconsin National Guard, brother Otto became secretary-treasurer of Pabst Brewing Co. Otto also organized Wisconsin Milling, making it become the largest corn products mill in the U.S.; helped form the Falk Corp., a steel casting plant; and was appointed the receiver of Allis-Chalmers' seven plants in 1911. In 1932 he emerged as Chairman of the Board of Allis-Chalmers, which at its peak, manufactured 1,600 different products and employed 18,000 people. Today, it no longer exists.

General Otto Falk

A typical large gear manufactured by the Falk Corp. Note the man standing beside this huge gear.

Falk manufactured street railway materials, heavy machinery, castings and was a pioneer in the development of power transmission devices.

On the opposite page is a photograph of one of Pawling and Harnischfeger's (P&H's) machine shops. They built electric cranes, power excavators, and mining equipment. In 1995, they had 14,000 employees worldwide and 1,900 employees in four local facilities. Following bankruptcy proceedings, the company emerged with a new name by which it is known today, Joy Global, Inc. Henry Harnischfeger came from Hesse, Germany to Milwaukee in 1881 and worked for the Whitehall Sewing Machine Company. He and Pawling then formed their partnership to become P&H. In 1930, shortly before his death, Henry Harnischfeger donated funds to Salmünster, Germany, for a school which bears his name, as does a major street in his hometown.

NORTH BAY MACHINE SHOP WEST

Koehring Company made commercial construction equipment for street paving and for the pulp and paper industry, along with manufacturing construction kerosene heaters, hydraulic hoe scoopers, excavators, crawlers, and truck mounted cranes.

During the 19th century, Milwaukee was one of many Wisconsin ports where wooden ships were built for transportation on the Great Lakes. The ship building industry later declined, but during WWII, it had a small revival in the Kinnickinnic River basin. Bernard Froeming was a native Milwaukeean who became involved in construction engineering. He received his first shipbuilding contract in 1941 and then converted 12 acres of unimproved land along the Kinnickinnic River into a shipyard – all in 60 days.

The Menomonee River Valley has canals which were dredged for boat accessibility to industries along its banks. Today, under the street viaducts, most industry is gone. Parkland is being developed.

Where the Milwaukee and Kinnickinnic Rivers met and flowed into Lake Michigan (later the Menomonee River was channeled to join them) there was a marshy island that was settled in 1870 by Kashubians and German immigrants.

The "Fisher Folk" earned their living by fishing and contributed to the economy by selling their fish on the mainland. They maintained a nearly self-sufficient community which remained virtually unchanged for decades. Having no deeds to their

properties, the "squatters" were evicted in 1940 from what is now known as Jones Island, currently home of the Port of Milwaukee and the primary wastewater treatment plant for the city of Milwaukee.

GERMAN PRINTING AND PUBLISHING

As early as 1844, printing machinery was built in Milwaukee by the early German settlers and newspapers were then printed in German for the immigrants. The first German newspaper, the *Wiskonsin Banner*, was published by pioneer journalist Moritz Schöffler (1844).

Newspapers covered a broad spectrum from socialist to conservative. Some editors greatly influenced the social climate of the time. Paul Grottkau, a German-born Socialist, published the *Arbeiter Zeitung* (Workers' Newspaper) and organized the Central Labor Union, lobbying for an eight-hour work day.

By 1876 half of Milwaukee's ten daily newspapers were published in German. Over the years, publishing firms included Brumder, Casper & Zahn, Hammerschmidt, Kalmbach, Moebius, and Wetzel Bros.

Assimilation into the American culture, as well as the anti-German sentiment following

William Coleman, born in Bremen, Germany, published the Herold, *which became the most popular German-language newspaper in the Midwest. George Brumder bought the Coleman papers in 1906.*

In the 1850s, Henry Seifert packed his wood press and some choice equipment and with all of it sailed to America. He took a train to Buffalo and went by ox cart to Chicago, then to Milwaukee by ship. He is important in the establishment of Die Lithographie *(Lithography). Lithography is a special printing process invented in Germany, which when brought to Milwaukee, produced the first prints in the state of Wisconsin. By 1870 steam-driven presses were brought to Milwaukee, and two lithography businesses with a dozen hand presses were employing 25 people; one, the Gugler Lithography Company, is shown above. (This, and other similar businesses, contributed to Milwaukee's reputation as a first-rate printing city.) So popular was the process that in 1892 five businesses had 32 steam presses, 50 hand presses, artists,* Gravueren *(engravers), printers, and 350 employees.*

In 1884, the Herold *and* Seebote *newspapers had a combined circulation of 92,000. The English language* Sentinel, Journal, *and* Evening Wisconsin *totaled half of that. By 1910 circulation dropped due to changes in urban lifestyle and immigration patterns. At one time, there were as many as ten German newspapers in Milwaukee.*

The German-language newspapers locally published in Milwaukee over the years included:

Wisconsin Banner
Seebote
Volksfreund
Atlas
Arbeiter
Phoenix
Forwärts
Milwaukee Freie Presse
Volksblatt
Der Reformer
Germania, Herold
Milwaukee Frauenzeitung
Abendpost
Milwaukee Sonntagspost
Milwaukee Deutsche Zeitung
Amerikanische Turnzeitung
Columbia
Duetsches Volksblatt
Korsar
Wahrheit
Nordwestliche Post
Humanist

WWI resulted in less German being spoken and, consequently, less need for German print material. German newspapers were no longer printed in Milwaukee after the *Milwaukee Deutsche Zeitung* (Milwaukee German Newspaper) ceased production in 1984.

George Brumder, from the Alsace region, was very involved with his family, his church, and his business. He began his career by publishing Lutheran tracts in the rear of his bookstore situated on the Milwaukee River. When the German Protestant Printing Association went bankrupt in 1874, he bought their Germania paper. He offered incentives for pre-paid yearly subscriptions in the form of books on current affairs, and eventually made a practice of acquiring troubled German newspapers in the Midwest throughout the years.

Due to increasing German immigration, readership of German-language newspapers in Milwaukee was twice that of English newspapers. When the Bennet Law, which required "English Only" in schools, passed in the legislature, Germans especially became angry and voted the Republicans from office. George Brumder, a Lincoln Republican, urged his readers to vote Democratic. He published a popular yearly almanac, a Sunday supplement entitled *Der Haus und Bauernfreund* (the Home and Farm Companion), and more than 400 books, mostly in German. In 1906, when he bought control of the *Herold*, he controlled all of the major Milwaukee German newspapers. He also owned German language papers in Chicago and Lincoln, Nebraska, as well as in several Milwaukee area towns.

Brumder had the foresight to realize that German-language publishing had little future in coming years, so he invested in other ventures and encouraged his sons to do so also. In 1910, he returned from a trip to Washington, D.C., for President Taft's inauguration, in poor physical condition, and just months later, he died.

Germania Building, Milwaukee, Wis.

In downtown Milwaukee, over the doorway of the Germania Building, was a ten-foot bronze statue of Germania, *a mythic symbol of Bismarck's 1871 united Germany. At the onset of the First World War, it was removed because of anti-German sentiment. The building name changed from* Germania *to the Brumder Building. The statue cannot be found today; some people believe it was melted for ordnance during WWII.*

George Brumder

This page from Die Nordamericanische Vogelwelt *(The North American Bird World) by Heinrich Nehrling, is George Brumder's most important publishing masterpiece. It was published in 1891 in two versions, German and English, and shows 36 color plates throughout the 637 pages.*

The frieze at the top of the Journal Building on State Street features the highlights of communication, such as the symbolic introduction of printing in Europe with the invention of movable type by Gutenberg. His invention stimulated the change from the hand-written manuscript to the mass production of the type-set printed page. The 19th century saw many innovations in printing-related processes, including, machine-made paper, rotary presses, and Linotype machines, the latter being first produced by German-born Ottmar Mergenthaler in 1886. The 20th century saw the move from letterpress to offset printing. Milwaukee firms participated in all of these innovations. Today Pewaukee-based Quadgraphics (20 miles west of Milwaukee) is the largest privately held printer/publisher in the Western hemisphere, printing numerous magazines such as *Time, Newsweek, Playboy, US News & World Report* and other national publications, thereby making Milwaukee one of the country's largest printing centers.

August Wetzel, a printer, was joined by his brother, Ignaz, a lithographer, to start a printing business of their own in 1885. Later, the business was incorporated (1899), and it is known today as Wetzel Brothers Printing, Inc.

William George Bruce (originally Bruss) came from New York. He became a reporter for the Milwaukee Sentinel, *established the* American School Board Journal and Industrial Arts *magazine. He fought the illegal diversion of lake waters into the Chicago Drainage Canal in 1922, and later served as chairman of the Harbor Commission. He is known for his Milwaukee history published by his Bruce Publishing Company.*

Peter V. Deuster published the Seebote (The Lake [Michigan] Messenger), *the leading Democratic newspaper in Wisconsin and was editor-in-chief from 1860 to 1904. A three-term congressman in the early 1880s, he secured the first appropriation for the inner harbor at Milwaukee.*

Roy Reiman, of German parentage, developed a publishing empire in 1965 in Greendale, (11.5 miles southwest of Milwaukee). The company, which has recently been sold to Reader's Digest, prints cookbooks, coffee table books, and 14 national magazines, including Taste of Home, *which is the largest food magazine in the world. It ranks sixth among all magazines published in the United States.*

GERMAN BUSINESSES

Many German immigrants came to Milwaukee with purpose, skills, determination and a strong desire to provide a better life for their families. They built houses and planted gardens. They worked, shared, traded services, and supplied products. Meatpackers sold animal hides to tan, while farmers brought grain to be milled into flour and barley for malting; and so evolved the three early major German-owned industries: tanning, milling, and brewing. These operations in turn required buildings wherein to work, basic machinery and subsequent repair and maintenance, containers, distribution facilities, and transportation for sales.

Everyone needed food, shoes, and clothing. Businesses were born to produce and sell. Banks and exchanges serviced the economy. Women kept house, laundered and sewed for their families and others. Visitors and travelers sought a place to stay, making hotels a necessity. The climate and the location afforded hills for storage of beer (in caves), and access to water (three rivers and the lake) for power and transport.

After the Civil War, the Industrial Revolution emerged at full force in Milwaukee.

East Wisconsin Avenue was the commercial center of downtown. Insurance companies, business offices, hotels, department stores, and the Federal Post Office lined the street.

Other options included laundering; many women took laundry into their homes, while others worked in commercial laundries such as this.

Female employment, although growing, was still limited to certain jobs. These telephone operators exemplify one choice for women at that time.

This "Carriage and Wagon Manufactory" of Haekler and Habhegger made buggies, sleighs, and wagons. Habhegger Wheel and Axel continues in business today on Water Street.

CANDY

Ambrosia Chocolate Company opened in 1894, and has been making and distributing chocolate all over the world ever since. Otto Schoenleber originally sold furniture and coffins, but turned to chocolate following the 1893 world financial panic. Like most major financial downturns, the depression of the 1890s was preceded by a series of shocks that undermined public confidence and weakened the economy. The depression of the 1890s did not fully abate until 1897; by this time, Ambrosia was a stable company. Later, Schoenleber switched to making bulk chocolate for large companies such as Hostess, Pillsbury, and Nabisco.

The original Ambrosia Company built its chocolate facility in downtown Milwaukee. In 1930, the county built the Milwaukee County Courthouse on that site. Otto Schoenleber's daughters, Marie and Louise, became Ambrosia directors and donated a clock tower which was erected in the courthouse plaza in memory of their parents, Otto and Emma. The clock has since been moved to another location.

Milwaukee candymakers Ambrosia and Ziegler both employed many women.

This Ambrosia picture is circa May 1909.

Wholesale candy manufacturers (photo below) supplied general stores (left photo) with confectionery delights. Kehr's Kandy Kitchen is a well-known Milwaukee chocolatier specializing in hand-dipped and holiday-themed chocolates since 1930. Today, they have expanded to include a second shop, Kehr's Candies, in the Milwaukee Public Market, that continues the company tradition.

A general store is festively decorated for a large sale.

If you grew up in Milwaukee in the 1950s or 1960s, you may remember the nickel Ziegler Giant Bar, a classic chocolate-peanut bar made by the local George Ziegler Candy Company. Mary Ziegler, who, with husband William, owns a candy store in West Allis (seven miles southwest of Milwaukee), and is the fifth generation of Ziegler candy makers. The Giant Bar first appeared in 1911. After WWII, the Ziegler Company started a Milwaukee tradition by donating two bars each Halloween to every schoolchild in Milwaukee. Although the George Ziegler Company went out of business in 1972, the Ziegler Giant Bars are still poured in patented molds and sold today by the Zieglers.

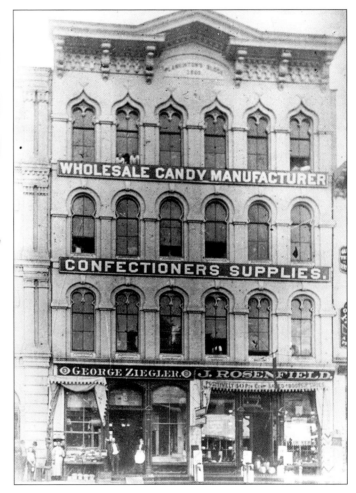

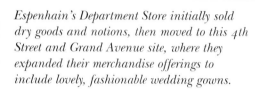

Espenhain's Department Store initially sold dry goods and notions, then moved to this 4th Street and Grand Avenue site, where they expanded their merchandise offerings to include lovely, fashionable wedding gowns.

The 12th Street Schuster's Store is pictured here. Their other two stores were on upper 3rd Street and on Mitchell Street. Santa Claus Parade floats moved on streetcar tracks on the evening before Thanksgiving. Meetok, the Eskimo, cared for Santa's reindeer at a garage at this store, and children came from all over the state to see them. Families would then visit Toyland inside the store so children could sit on Santa's lap and whisper their Christmas wishes. Later, Gimbel's acquired Schuster's and then Marshall Field's (now owned by Macy's) took over Gimbel's.

In this German shopping district, the busy intersection of upper 3rd Street and North Avenue, were Schuster's Department Store, Welke's House of Roses, Eitel's Picture Framing Shop, Hess Butcher Shop, Kornely Hardware, First Wisconsin National Bank, Margaret's Bakery, Bitker-Gerner Ladies Dress Shop, Günther's Grocery Store, and Brill's Men's Clothier. On the far left, in the photo below, was Rosenberg's, a popular, high-end women's fashion center. The interior of Rosenberg's is shown on the right. Milwaukee never enjoyed a richly expanded and full downtown like most cities, because there were three major shopping districts (upper 3rd Street, 12th and Vliet, and Mitchell Street). Schuster's was an anchor in each.

Otto Reckmeyer was a prominent downtown Milwaukee furrier.

John Droegkamp Company is still in business selling furnaces and air conditioners. Sheet metal furnaces were an innovative necessity to keep warm in the cold Wisconsin winters.

Toepfer owned this iron works business. He was considered a lock genius and built an early automobile.

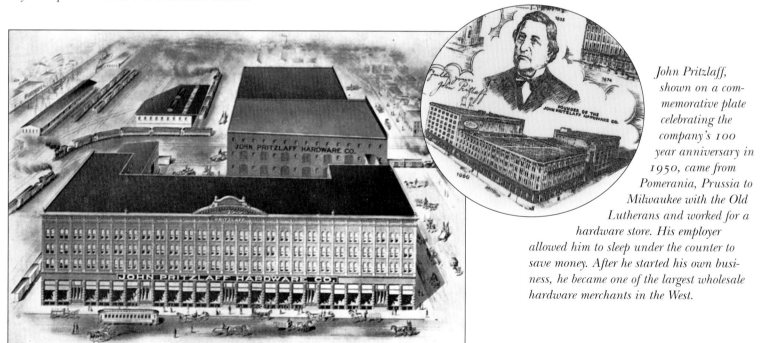

John Pritzlaff, shown on a commemorative plate celebrating the company's 100 year anniversary in 1950, came from Pomerania, Prussia to Milwaukee with the Old Lutherans and worked for a hardware store. His employer allowed him to sleep under the counter to save money. After he started his own business, he became one of the largest wholesale hardware merchants in the West.

The shoe business in Milwaukee grew quickly when they stopped making shoes by hand and began using machines.

Grassler and Gezelschap were manufacturers of gas and electric chandeliers, and plumbing and heating fixtures.

Mieselbach Bicycle Factory in North Milwaukee supplied bicycles for children and adults. Cycling was a popular sport and mode of transportation before automobiles.

Jack Donges had his shop for hats and gloves on 3rd and State streets in downtown Milwaukee. He married Fred Usinger's daughter, Louise.

Hatters provided derbies, straw boaters, caps and cowboy hats for the fashion-conscious man. For women, milliners sold hats with wide brims, bows, tulle and even birds for decoration. Fresh flowers could be incorporated into the designs as well.

Hats, ties, and removable collars were essential for the businessman. Indeed, all men wore hats, even to picnics and other social occasions.

The Ragman was a welcome fixture who collected papers, cardboard and rags. His call of "Rags! Bottles! Iron!" echoed in the air. We hurried to him with our discards.

Der Scherenschleifer *(the scissors grinder) traveled the neighborhoods to sharpen scissors, knives, axes and other tools. "Watch the sparks!"*

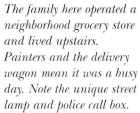

The family here operated a neighborhood grocery store and lived upstairs. Painters and the delivery wagon mean it was a busy day. Note the unique street lamp and police call box.

This scene shows the northwest corner of Wisconsin Avenue and 3rd Street. On the sky-line, the City Hall tower, the Germania Building's "Kaiser's Helmet," and (to the left) the distinctive brickwork on the still-standing Wisconsin Hotel can be seen.

Here yesterday, gone today: Donges Hats is now a sandwich shop, the buildings on the right were demolished for Pere Marquette Park, the streetcars are gone and so is this block of Plankinton Avenue. Here "the streetcar bends the corner around."

A. Schoenleber's furniture store, circa 1854

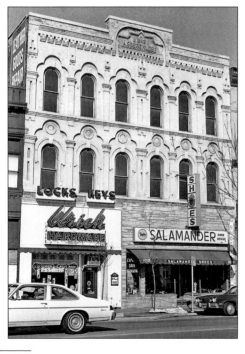

William Upmeyer   *Louis Bunde*

The Salamander Shoe Store on Old World Third Street was popular with later German immigrants because it carried a selection of imported German shoes.

Louis Bunde and his partner, William Upmeyer, known as BillyUp, founded Bunde & Upmeyer Jewelers on Wisconsin Avenue in Milwaukee at the turn of the 20th century, and became the state's largest jewelry retailer. Their office in New York City dealt only in fresh water pearls found in the rivers of Wisconsin. They also had a dental laboratory and a stationery business.

German Businesses | HISTORY

ICE

Wisconsin's cold winters yielded ice from its many lakes, rivers and marshes. Brewers and citizens alike welcomed the ice, as it was, prior to mechanical refrigeration, essential both for the lager-making process and for the preservation of food. John H. Kopmeier's father came from Germany to Cincinnati, where John earned twenty five cents a day. In 1849, after a move to Milwaukee, John worked for "Ice Bear" Kroeger and loaded ice wagons by hand (before tongs). When a later employer was short of cash, and could not pay Kopmeier his wages, he deeded a hilly lot to Kopmeier to liquidate his debt. Kopmeier took the property, dug a hole in the hill for storing ice, and supplied customers year-round. His son, Norman, married Loretta Miller and another son, Waldemar, married Meta Uihlein, both daughters of brewers. In 1880, Blatz built an ice-house and used 30,000 tons of ice that year, much of it from Kopmeier's company, Wisconsin Ice and Coal.

Above the dam where the water was known to be especially clean and clear, men are cutting big blocks of ice from the Milwaukee River. The dam was removed in the 1980s to renew the natural flow of water.

Large saws cut blocks of ice to be delivered. Children followed the ice trucks hoping for chips. Customers displayed a card in their windows to show how many pounds of ice they needed that day. Hand-held tongs were used to carry the ice safely into the icebox. Inside the icebox, melt water ran down a tube and collected in a pan. "Empty the pan before it overflows!"

Theo Vilter was president of Vilter Manufacturing Co. which manufactured early mechanical refrigeration.

J. H. Kopmeier incorporated his ice business as Wisconsin Ice and Coal.

Edward Uhrig was the President of Milwaukee Fuel Company.

August Bergenthal was one of the founders of Red Star Yeast Company. Red Star Yeast is still available today.

Otto Pietsch operated a chemical dye works for fabrics used in manufacturing clothing.

The fine cigar leaf type of tobacco that prospered in Wisconsin soil and the high demand, chiefly by Wisconsin's German residents, made the cigar business very profitable. In 1912 there were 217 cigar manufacturers in the city. Henry Rolfs, an early cigar manufacturer in Milwaukee until 1895, moved to West Bend (40 miles northwest of Milwaukee), where his descendants founded Amity-Rolfs Leather Products, a thriving business today.

In 1939, Jack Uhle established his tobacco business which he acquired from R. Spiegel, another German immigrant, who rolled and sold his own cigars. Highly regarded, Uhle is known as Wisconsin's premier tobacconist. He first manufactured his own blends of tobacco for pipes and then expanded into private labels for cigars. Since 1954 Uhle's Pipe Shop has been located on Wisconsin Avenue between the Riverside Theater and the Milwaukee River.

Frederick Kasten was born in 1855 in Milwaukee to parents from Bremen, Germany. He was one of the organizers of the Wisconsin National Bank and served as its first cashier. Kasten and the Turners' Frankfurter Riege (team) competed in Frankfurt and surprised the Germans by winning most of the gymnastics prizes. Fred and the boys received an Olympic-style reception at home.

William Brumder, son of publisher George Brumder, was a UW-Madison graduate and a member of its first football team. He married Thekla Uihlein in 1900 in the Pfister Hotel ballroom. After his father died in 1910, he took over the Germania newspapers. Later, he and Thekla bought the Schlesinger family home on Lake Drive, which is now the Hefter Center of UW-Milwaukee.

The Second Ward Bank was known as the Brewers' bank because the Best, Schlitz, and Uihlein families banked there. Initially, it was a bank for the German neighborhood surrounding it. Due to a consolidation it became the First Wisconsin National Bank in 1929 (on right in above photo), which later donated the building to the Milwaukee County Historical Society. This view looks west on Kilbourn Avenue prior to the construction of the Milwaukee County Courthouse. Today it is restored (above right) and welcomes the public with displays of donated historical materials, a large library of pictures, immigrant information and a colorful lighting display in the evenings.

USINGER'S

Frederick Usinger, Sr., came from Hesse, Germany, where he had apprenticed as a butcher. He had spent his *Wanderjahr* (journeyman year) visiting other butchers and collecting recipes. At age 19 he arrived in Milwaukee with $400 in cash and those recipes. He went to work in Mrs. Gärtner's Butcher Shop, and in a year had married her niece, Louise. He later bought the shop and they moved into the quarters upstairs. Their sausage business is still operated on the same site by the fourth generation Usinger family.

Even the women could push around these marble carts. A Usinger slogan of the late twentieth century, Usinger's: "America's feinste Würste … Ja! Ja! Ja! Ja!" (Usinger's: America's finest sausage).

Wurstmacher *(sausage maker)* Frederick Usinger, Sr.

This horse-drawn cart was used for local delivery. Today, a shipping center on the near south side of Milwaukee supplies mail order sausage to the entire United States.

"Die feinste Wurst ist jedem Deutschen wohl behagen." (The finest sausage suits every German well.)

The clerks used to speak in German; today only a few still do.

Men and women alike wore coverings on their heads in the Usinger packaging assembly line.

The 1880s flavor is still evident today in the retail store, fixtures, and wall murals. The only "update" is a take-a-number device.

George Peter came to Milwaukee from Germany to paint animals on the Panoramas. He also painted the mural of elves making sausages which surrounds the Usinger sales room and can be seen today. Known as the "Usinger Elves," they were used in marketing and advertising campaigns and are remembered fondly. Zum Schluss der Wurst ein Kräftig "Hoch!" Mög sie lang'uns schmecken noch. (In closing, a hearty toast to the sausage, may it long taste good to us!)

The Pabst Theater is one of the most beautiful theaters in the United States. Today, The Pabst Theater is the centerpiece of Milwaukee's downtown theater district... a magnificent example of architecture of another time and era that serves performers and audiences of the 21st century as it did at the turn of the 20th century.

At the turn of the century, as today, people loved to watch parades. This parade, down Wisconsin Avenue, shows a festively decorated Plankinton Building and cars, parade onlookers and even the streetcar as it travels toward Gimbel's.

FAMILY RECIPES

ZUCKER BREZELN
(PRETZEL-SHAPED SUGAR COOKIES)

INGREDIENTS

1 1/2 cups sugar
2 sticks butter
4 egg yolks
4 cups all purpose
flour, divided
1 lemon peel, grated

KATHLEEN KENNY ARENZ

Preheat the oven to 350 degrees. Mix the sugar and the butter together with a fork. Be careful not to cream. Add the lemon rind. Mix in the egg yolks by hand, gradually adding 3 cups flour. Use up to an additional 1/3 cup of flour if the egg yolks are large.

Divide the cookie dough into 3 inch balls and individually roll out on a lightly floured surface, using remaining 2/3 cup flour as needed. Make each ball of dough 8 to 10 inches long. Shape into pretzels and place on an ungreased cookie sheet. Bake at 350 degrees for eight minutes.

Hints: Rinse your hands in cold water. If your hands get hot, the dough will not keep its pretzel shape. Try to make one cookie first to see if it comes out right. Add more flour or egg yolk to the dough if necessary.

If desired, decorate the knot of the pretzel with slivers of red and green cherries to make your dessert look like a Christmas bow.

MAKES 36

My great-great-grandfather, Bernhardt Wey, emigrated from Wasungen Germany in Thuringia to Milwaukee in 1849. He tried his hand at farming in the Sheboygan area, operated a tavern on Watertown Plank Road in Milwaukee, and later owned a general store in Sauk City.

His letters home to Germany were quite descriptive, and tell of bears, wildcats and wolves in the countryside and the bustling commerce and entrepreneurship in the cities. His letters were also filled with accounts of local customs and happenings. He was impressed by the Americans' drive to "make new wealth" by starting new businesses, taking risks and constantly moving from place to place.

Bernhardt Wey's grand-daughter was my grandmother Edith Wey Kenny. These cookies were a family favorite. At Christmas she would decorate them with red and green maraschino cherries or bits of citron. Despite having an electric mixer, she always mixed the ingredients by hand.

SCHNECKEN (SNAIL SHAPED SWEET ROLLS)

EDITH HOFFMANN

My mother was great at baking and cooking, but short on recipes. When I asked her about what goes into a particular dish, her favorite response was, "Ach, you know, a bit of this and that!" So, I made dishes by trial and error; she made them by heart. Being a modern woman, I added a few shortcuts, like dough mix, so my recipe is easy to follow. My Oma made *Schnecken* for her family in Germany. My mother made them for her family; I make them for my family, and my daughter, Nancy, makes them for her family. Perhaps the fifth generation will carry on our sweet little tradition.

INGREDIENTS

TOPPING
1 cup brown sugar
1 cup raisins
1 cup chopped walnuts
1 Tbsp. cinnamon
1 tsp. nutmeg

DOUGH
4 cups all-purpose flour
1 pkg. active dry yeast
1 cup milk
1/4 cup sugar
1/4 cup shortening
1 tsp. salt
2 eggs

OR

1 box Pillsbury Hot Roll mix

For homemade dough, combine two cups of flour and one package of active dry yeast in a large mixing bowl. Heat one cup of milk, 1/4 cup of sugar, 1/4 cup of shortening, and one teaspoon of salt, until warm. Stir the mixture to melt the shortening and slowly add to the dry ingredients in the bowl. Add two eggs. Beat at a low speed with the mixer for 30 seconds, scraping the sides of the bowl. Beat for three minutes on high setting. Stir in 1 to 2 cups of flour, by hand, to make moderately stiff dough. Knead the dough on a lightly floured surface for 8 to 10 minutes, or until smooth. Shape the dough into a ball and place in a greased bowl, turning once, to coat with oil. Cover and let rise for 45 to 60 minutes, or until the ball doubles in size. Punch down and divide the dough in half. Cover and let the dough rest for 10 minutes. Roll the dough onto a board and continue with preparation as described below.

Preheat the oven to 375 degrees. Mix the dry topping ingredients together and set aside. Melt three tablespoons of butter in a cup and reserve. Shape the dough by cutting the ball in half. Roll half of the dough out on a lightly floured board into a rectangle roughly 10 by 15 inches. Cover with half of the melted butter and half of the topping mixture. Roll the dough tightly from the long side and press edges to seal. Cut into 15 slices. Place the slices cut-side down on a large cookie sheet sprayed with Pam. Repeat the process for the other half of the dough and ingredients. Cover loosely with plastic wrap and towel and let the *Schnecken* rise for 20 to 30 minutes. Bake at 375 degrees for 15 to 20 minutes, or until golden brown. Remove the *Schnecken* from the pan and place on a rack to cool.

MAKES 30 SCHNECKENS

WURSTSALAT GARNIERT
(GARNISHED SAUSAGE SALAD)

INGREDIENTS

5 Knackwurst, fully cooked

3-1/2 oz. Gruyere or Emmentaler cheese

2 gherkins

1/2 small white onion

1 large tomato

1 hard-boiled egg, cooled, peeled

4 or 5 chives, chopped

VINAIGRETTE

1/2 tsp. Grey Poupon mustard

1/4 tsp. Knorr Aromat

A few drops of Maggi Swiss seasoning

4 Tbsp. tarragon vinegar

3 Tbsp. canola oil

A pinch of white pepper

A pinch of garlic salt

Skin the fully cooked Knackwurst sausages and cut in half lengthwise, slicing into thin pieces. Cut the cheese into strips and add to the Knackwurst.

To make the vinaigrette, chop the gherkins and onion finely and set aside. Whisk together the remaining ingredients for the vinaigrette. Add onions, gherkins and some chives to the vinaigrette and pour over the salad. Toss well to coat. Slice the tomatoes and hard-boiled egg and arrange on top. Chill well. Garnish the salad with your favorite greens and top with fresh chives. Serve with crusty bread or rolls. Preparation time is 30 to 45 minutes.

SERVES 4

ELLA AESCHBACK

My family is originally from Thun, Switzerland. In 1967, we moved to Milwaukee for my husband's job, before settling in New Berlin. I brought along many of my favorite recipes, including Wurstsalat Garniert, or sausage salad. It is a classic dish known to cure the homesickness of many expatriate Swiss-Germans. The salad is great for lunch or a light supper, especially in the summer months. It is also very good for outdoor gatherings. Just keep the salad cool until it is time to eat. This is one of the first lunches my husband orders when we visit Switzerland. All the village inns serve their own unique version.

SCHWEINEBRATEN UND ROT KOHL
(PORK ROAST AND RED CABBAGE)

PORK ROAST		RED CABBAGE	
3-4 lbs. pork roast	oil	2 lbs. red cabbage	2 red apples, pared, cored and chopped
5 cloves garlic	salt	1/2 tsp. cloves	1/4 cup vinegar
onions	pepper	1/2 cup sugar	1/4 cup butter
beef base	cornstarch	cornstarch	

ELSIE MAE ARENZ

My father came to the United States from Austria/Yugoslovia in 1917. He joined the American Army and became a mess sergeant, so he was very comfortable in the kitchen. He was sent to Germany after World War I, where he met my mother, a German civilian nurse in the American Red Cross. They married and came to the United States in 1924. Both of my parents shared a strong Germanic food background and became excellent cooks. Pork dishes were a mainstay in our family of eight children. We always had plenty of fresh vegetables from our large garden. As children, we all learned how to cook many German dishes.

Pork Roast:

Preheat the oven to 400 degrees. Cut four to five slits into the top of the roast. Rub the roast with a little oil. Sprinkle salt and pepper over the top of the roast. Place garlic in the slits. Slice the onions into wedges and place on top and on the sides of the roast. Place the pork fatty side up in a shallow pan. Brown the roast uncovered at 400 degrees for 45 minutes. Reduce the temperature to 350 degrees and continue roasting for 1-2 hours, or until the temperature inside the roast reaches 185 degrees. Place the roast on a warm platter. Break up the cooked onions and add water and beef base to the shallow pan.

Bring the mixture to a boil. In a separate bowl, add water to the cornstarch to make a paste. Then, add the starch to the mixture to thicken it to the consistency of gravy.

Red Cabbage:

Remove any outer wilted cabbage leaves, then rinse cabbage head and cut it into quarters. Coarsely shred the cabbage, discarding the core. Put the cabbage in a heavy pot, and add the chopped apples, sugar, vinegar and cloves. Cook for about 15 minutes or until the cabbage and apples are tender. Stir in butter and thicken with cornstarch and water paste.

SERVES 6 TO 8

SAUERBRATEN

INGREDIENTS:

4 to 5 lb. beef rump roast
1/4 cup canola oil
6 Tbsp. all-purpose flour
4 Tbsp. salted butter
3/4 cup seedless raisins
3/4 cup sour cream
1 tsp. salt
1/4 tsp. black pepper

MARINADE:

3 cups white vinegar
3 cups water
3 medium yellow onions, sliced
1 branch celery, chopped
1 medium carrot, chopped
3 bay leaves
12 peppercorns, crushed
12 whole cloves
1/2 tsp. mustard seed

GINGER FORSTER

My father, Erwin Plonus, came to the United States from Prussia when he was seven. My mother's family came from Frankfurt. So, I was raised in a home with a strong Germanic background. Growing up, I loved to cook, but I was always a little hesitant to cook without following a recipe. I was inspired to try more complicated German recipes after I got a German cookbook. It was much easier for me to use the book than to learn from someone who tells you to "add a little of this" and "a little bit of that." I hope this book encourages everyone to try German cooking!

To make the marinade, combine the vinegar, water, onions, celery, carrot, bay leaves, peppercorns, cloves and mustard seed in a saucepan. Bring the ingredients to a boil and remove from heat and allow to cool. Place the meat in a large bowl and pour the marinade over the meat. Cover tightly and place in the refrigerator. Allow the roast to marinate for two to three days, turning several times. Remove the meat from the marinade and dry well. Save the marinade. Sprinkle the meat with salt and pepper. On the stovetop, heat the oil in a deep roasting pot. Brown the meat well on all sides. Add three cups of the marinade to the pot. Cover and let the roast simmer for two to three hours or until the meat is very tender. Remove the roast and keep it warm. Strain the solids from the sauce. Skim off the fat with a spoon and measure the liquid. Add water or leftover marinade to the sauce to make four cups. Brown all-purpose flour and butter in a skillet, making a roux. Stir browned flour into the sauce made from the combination of roasting liquids and marinade. Cook the sauce over low heat, stirring and scraping browned bits, until desired thickness is reached. Stir in raisins and sour cream, mixing well. Slice the meat and serve with the sauce. Add more raisins and sour cream, if desired.

SERVES 6

CORNELIA ILLE

Growing up, I learned how to cook from my mother, Gerda Ille, and her mother, Anna Jahnke, or "Mutti," as she became known to all. Mutti was born in 1908 in the small town of Meissdorf in the Harz Mountain region of Lower Saxony. She was the only one of her seven siblings to venture beyond the region. She moved to Berlin between World War I and World War II and became a cook. There she met my grandfather, and they started a family. They lost all their possessions during World War II.

In 1952, my grandparents emigrated to the United States with their two teenage children. Mutti came to this country to start a new life at 44 years old, speaking only a little English, and carrying few possessions. The only recipe book she brought with her was the one in her heart. In all the years I have watched her cook, I have never seen her use a written recipe. As she got older, I started taking notes to preserve the recipes. You will notice that I use the words "to taste" quite frequently. It was Mutti's way of cooking, and it tasted the best!

BEEF ROULADEN

INGREDIENTS

*8 - 10 thin slices of beef
(1/4 inch thick and about
the size of your hand)
Stone ground mustard
Dill pickles, sliced lengthwise
8 - 10 slices of bacon
2 - 3 medium white onions, sliced*

*1 large carrot, chopped
2 - 3 bay leaves
All-purpose flour (for gravy),
mixed with 1 cup of water
3 cups beef stock
Salt and black pepper to taste
Toothpicks, metal skewers or string*

Preheat the oven to 375 degrees. Tenderize the slices of beef with a meat hammer. Take each piece of meat and spread the mustard on one side. Lay one piece of bacon, a few slices of onion and a slice of a small pickle in the middle of each meat slice. Sprinkle with salt and pepper to taste. Roll the meat so it surrounds the bacon, onion, and pickle. Use toothpicks, metal skewers or string to secure the rolled meat. Brown the Rouladen in a pan. Transfer them to a deep roasting pan, adding water or beef stock to cover the bottom of the pan. Also add any leftover onions and carrots. Cover the pan with foil and place in the oven. Bake at 375 degrees for 1 - 2 hours, or until the meat is tender. Baste the Rouladen every 15 minutes, adding water or beef stock as necessary.

Remove the cooked Rouladen, and place them on a serving dish. Keep warm. Leave the leftover juices in the pan to make a gravy. Add the flour mixed with water to the sauce in the skillet. Stir over low heat to the consistency you prefer. Run the gravy through a sieve to remove the remaining chunks of carrots and onions. Serve with red cabbage and dumplings (see other recipes).

SERVES 6 TO 8

PORK SCHNITZEL (BREADED PORK CUTLET)

INGREDIENTS

*1 1/2 lbs. pork shoulder or pork
  butt, sliced and pounded thin*
1/2 cup all-purpose flour
3 large eggs, lightly beaten
1 cup fine dry bread crumbs
1 tsp. hot seasoned salt

1 tsp. garlic salt
1 tsp. seasoned salt
3 Tbsp. olive oil
3 Tbsp. butter
1 lemon, cut into wedges

Preheat the olive oil in a large skillet and add butter. Heat until the butter is no longer foamy. In three separate shallow dishes place flour, eggs, and bread crumbs. Add the hot seasoned salt, seasoned salt and garlic salt to the bread crumbs. Dredge the pounded pork schnitzels in the flour, shake off the excess, dip in eggs and coat them in bread crumbs. Place fillets directly into hot skillet, one at a time. Brown for approximately four minutes on each side. Transfer the fillets to a plate lined with paper towels to absorb the excess grease. Keep the schnitzels warm in a 250 degree oven, until you are ready to serve. Garnish with a lemon wedge. Serve with potatoes or dumplings.

SERVES 4-6

BOB FORSTER

Pork Schnitzel finds its roots in the world famous Wiener Schnitzel, which is made of veal, and, as its German language name hints, is associated with the City of Vienna. The historical origins of the dish are a matter of an intra-family dispute, in that both the Austrian and Italian branches of the royal Hapsburg dynasty claimed credit for the culinary invention. Whatever the origins of this delicious dish, there is no doubt that schnitzel's became very popular in German-speaking lands including Wisconsin.

WEIHNACHTS STOLLEN
(CHRISTMAS STOLLEN)

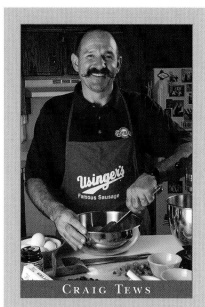

CRAIG TEWS

I got my love of yeast dough from my mother, who at age 11 won a local 4-H cooking demonstration by preparing bread before an audience. I was the same age when mom went back to work, and not wanting me to come home from school and plant myself in front of the TV, she would leave me instructions to finish dinner which she had partially prepared in the morning.

This eventually progressed to making *Stollen,* a sweet yeast bread filled with candied fruit and raisins at Christmas time. I've made changes over the years to make the recipe my own, such as adding cardamom and anise seed to the spices. I also use quick rise yeast to speed up the process, although I still hand grind my cardamom and anise in a porcelain mortar and pestle. I've recently even started to grind my own wheat for flour.

Every year I make a number of *Stollens* to give to loved ones during the holiday season. For my family and friends, Christmas breakfast wouldn't be the same without our *Stollen.*

Scald 2-1/4 cups of milk and pour into a large mixing bowl. Add butter and mix with milk until melted. Add 1 cup of all-purpose flour, all the sugar and salt, then the yeast and stir. Add eggs and beat well, adding three cups of the flour to the mixture. Place in a larger buttered mixing bowl. Cover and let it rise until it has doubled in size, or about 45 minutes.

Place dough back into the original mixing bowl and add cardamom seed, anise, fruit, and stir. Add enough flour so that the dough pulls away from the sides of the bowl. The dough should remain a bit sticky. Knead for about 5 min-utes. Place the dough ball into a buttered bowl. Cover the bowl and let the dough rise until it has doubled in size. On a floured surface, knead the dough for about five minutes, then divide into 6 pieces. Knead each piece and shape into an oval loaf. Place loaves on a greased cookie sheet and brush with melted butter. Let the loaves rise for 20 minutes. Bake at 350 degrees for 30 minutes. Brush with butter while they are still warm.

For the icing, beat ingredients until smooth. After the loaves have cooled, about 20 minutes, frost with icing. Decorate with candied cherries.

MAKES 6 LOAVES

INGREDIENTS

2 1/4 cups milk
3/4 cup sugar
2 1/2 tsp. salt
2 1/4 sticks butter
2 pkg. quick-rising yeast
5 eggs
8 cups all-purpose flour
1/2 tsp. finely ground anise
3/4 tsp. finely ground cardamom (approximately 15 seeds)
1 1/2 cups finely chopped raisins
1 1/2 cups finely chopped candied fruit

ICING

4 cups powdered sugar
1 Tbsp. white vanilla
1 Tbsp. white rum
1/2 tsp. salt
1/4 cup melted butter
2 Tbsp. milk

KOENIGSBERGER KLOPSE
(MEATBALLS IN LEMON SAUCE)

MEATBALLS
1 1/2 lbs. ground beef
1 large white onion, chopped
1 egg
1 cup bread crumbs
1/4 cup milk
1 tsp. salt
1/2 tsp. black pepper

LEMON SAUCE
8 cups water
3 beef bouillon cubes
5 peppercorns, whole
1 bay leaf
Juice of 1/2 lemon
3 Tbsp. capers
1/2 cup cornstarch, dissolved in 1/2 cup cold milk
1/2 cup sour cream

Combine the meatball ingredients in a bowl, mixing by hand. Shape the meat into two inch meatballs and set aside. In a large pot, bring the water, beef bouillon, peppercorns and bay leaf to a boil. Stir the mixture until bouillon cubes are dissolved. Gently drop the meatballs into the sauce and reduce to a simmer. Cook for 15 to 20 minutes, or until the meatballs rise to the top. Remove the meatballs and keep them warm. Remove the peppercorns and the bay leaf and discard. Add the lemon juice, capers, and cornstarch to the pot. Bring the mixture to a boil, stirring constantly until it is slightly thickened. Remove 1 cup of the sauce and blend with 1/2 cup of sour cream, then return it to the mixture. Return the meatballs to the sauce and heat them thoroughly. Serve *Koenigsberger Klopse* over boiled potatoes or buttered noodles.

SERVES 6

INGEBORG JOHNSON

Since I was born in the East Prussian city of Koenigsberg, now Kaliningrad, this recipe for Koenigsberger Klopse holds special meaning for me. When our family emigrated to the United States in 1952, we settled in Cedarburg. My father, Erich Voss, worked as a sausage maker and butcher at Paulus Super Market in Cedarburg, while my mother, Herta, was in charge of the household.

When I was young, I would help my mother prepare this dish for our family. It was one of our favorite meals and continues to be a favorite with my relatives in Germany today.

KAREN RINALDI

My mother, Charlotte Badzio, a German immigrant, served this beef dish to our family in Milwaukee because it was quick, easy and nourishing. It can be used as a stew or a soup, with brown gravy, and is usually served during the winter months. As a young girl, my mother prepared *Gulasch* and called it *Gulasch Popochen* for fun. In German, *Popochen* means "little bottom." She is from the Pomeranian region in old East Germany, where potatoes were in abundant supply. So with the *Gulasch*, she would serve *Stampfkartoffeln*, or boiled potatoes, which are mashed potatoes with butter, milk, salt and pepper. She would use the *Gulasch* gravy for on top of the potatoes. This beef dish also goes well with red cabbage.

GULASCH POPOCHEN

INGREDIENTS

2 lbs. beef round steak, or stew meat, cut
   into 1/2 inch cubes
1 cup yellow onion, chopped (the more the better)
1 clove garlic, minced (my mom did not use garlic)
2 Tbsp. all-purpose flour
1 1/2 tsp. paprika

1/4 tsp. thyme, dried and crushed
1 bay leaf
1 can (14-1/2 oz.) whole tomatoes, peeled and diced
1 cup sour cream
1 tsp. salt and 1/2 tsp. black pepper to taste

This recipe can be cooked in 1-1/2 hours on the stovetop. You may have to add water. Put the steak cubes, onion, garlic in an oiled pan. Brown steak cubes well. Stir in flour and mix to coat steak cubes well. Add all remaining ingredients to the pot, except the sour cream, and stir well. Cover and cook slowly on low heat on the stovetop. Add the sour cream 30 minutes prior to serving, mixing thoroughly. Serve the beef and gravy over peeled, boiled potatoes or mashed potatoes, called *Stampfkartoffeln* in German.

There are many variations of this dish. Some cooks add carrots and celery. So, feel free to experiment and find the right taste for you and your family. Keep in mind this German proverb: *"Ein guter Koch ist ein Guter Artzt"* (A good cook is a good doctor). *Guten Appetit!*

SERVES 4-6

KARTOFFEL KLÖSE (POTATO DUMPLINGS)

INGREDIENTS
3 lbs. russet potatoes
12 oz. potato starch
3 Tbsp. salt
1/3 cup water
3 pieces of white bread,
*   toasted and cubed*

MARIANNA LUTHER

The day before I plan to serve the dumplings, I precook the potatoes. Boil the potatoes in their jackets in a large pot of water and drain. Allow the potatoes to cool until the next day, but do not refrigerate. When you are ready to prepare the dumplings, heat a large pot filled about two-thirds full with water. Add two tablespoons of salt to the water and bring to a simmering boil. Peel and rice the potatoes into a bowl. Add the potato starch and one tablespoon of salt, mixing carefully by hand. Add up to a 1/3 cup of water to make a dough consistency.

Form the dough into medium-sized balls, approximately three inches in diameter. While holding the formed dumpling, use a finger to make a small hole in the top of the dough. Fill the hole with a few bread cubes, and close the dumpling. The bread cubes make the dumpling light and fluffy. Carefully drop the dumplings into the simmering water. Dumplings will go to the bottom and rise to the top when they are done. Keep the water just simmering, and avoid rolling boil. Dumplings should be done in 20 to 25 minutes. Remove the dumplings from the pot with a slotted spoon and place them on a warm platter. If desired, garnish with parsley. Serve immediately.

SERVES 8 TO 10

(pictured here with Red Cabbage & Roast Pork)

I have fond memories of growing up on a farm, in a region called Franconia in northern Bavaria. Cooking was done with homegrown produce and meats. Our Sunday dinners were served promptly at noon. They consisted of a beef or pork roast with gravy, dumplings, vegetables, and fruit compote for dessert. My mother, Erma, was very particular about setting the table with beautiful linens, which were passed down as family heirlooms. We would spend Sunday afternoons going for a walk or visiting with relatives. Between 3:00 p.m. and 4:00 p.m. would be *Kaffee-Stunde*, coffee hour, where we enjoyed coffee and delicious homemade cakes.

Each region of Germany has its own dumpling specialty, so different recipes abound. Dumplings may be made from cooked potatoes alone, or from cooked and raw grated potatoes mixed together. They can be made by adding all-purpose flour, a little semolina, and sometimes an egg mixed into the dough. Bread dumplings are also very popular in many areas of Germany. I have chosen an easy to prepare recipe that always turns out great *Kartoffel Klöse*.

MARIA ABT

As a young girl I can remember my mother and grandmother preparing this dish with their own homemade noodles. It was sometimes served twice a week, especially in late fall when the family's chickens were young and tender.

HAENDEL PAPRIKASH
(CHICKEN PAPRIKA)

INGREDIENTS

1 chicken cut into pieces
3 Tbsp. vegetable or olive oil
3 medium or 2 large onions, diced
1 large tomato, chopped
1 large red or yellow bell pepper, chopped

1 small hot pepper
2 tsp. salt
1/8 tsp. black pepper
2 Tbsp. mild paprika
3 to 4 medium potatoes, peeled and cut into wedges

In a soup kettle or Dutch oven sauté onions in hot oil until lightly browned. Add paprika, tomato, peppers, and spices. Cook for 1 minute. Add chicken pieces and place potato wedges on top of chicken. Add just enough water to cover potatoes. Bring to a boil, then reduce heat and cook for 45 minutes or until chicken is done. Serve over home-style noodles.

SERVES 4

APFELSTRUDEL (APPLE STRUDEL)

INGREDIENTS
STRUDEL DOUGH

3 cups flour
Dash of salt
3 eggs (extra large or jumbo)
3 Tbsp. unsalted butter, not melted
6-9 Tbsp. water

FILLING

7-9 lbs. tart baking apples, peeled and sliced fine
Breadcrumbs, plain
12 Tbsp. sugar (for each)
Cinnamon
9-12 Tbsp. sour cream (3-5 Tbsp. for each)
Raisins (optional)

Put flour on the counter or on a board. Make a nest and mix salt, eggs and butter (soft, not melted) into the flour. Knead and add water until the dough becomes smooth. It should not stick to your hands. Let the dough rest for about a half hour covered with a bowl while you peel and slice the apples.

Cut the dough into 3 equal parts. Sprinkle a little flour on the board or countertop and start rolling. Roll each one paper-thin and place it on a cloth-covered table and let it dry for 20-30 minutes. Once each sheet of *Strudel* dough is rolled out, sprinkle breadcrumbs (small handful) to soak up some of the apple juices. Add 1/3 of the sliced apples and spread evenly. Sprinkle with 4 Tbsp. sugar and cinnamon to taste. Drizzle 3 to 5 Tbsp. sour cream over the apples and add raisins (optional).

Roll up as tight as possible and place on a 1x10x15 greased baking pan. Three *Strudels* fit nicely on one pan. Brush each strudel with melted butter and sprinkle with additional sugar and place in preheated oven. Bake 25 minutes at 425 degrees, then an additional 35 minutes at 350 degrees. When done, they should be golden brown and flaky on the top. Let *Strudel* cool and serve with vanilla ice cream or whipped cream.

SERVES 12

MARIANNE CLARE

Fall was and still is the time for *Strudel*, with plenty of good baking apples available. My mom made the best *Strudel*, maybe because we were so hungry for it. She never measured anything; she just knew how much and when it was right. I don't remember seeing any measuring tools or gadgets in our kitchen.

As a little girl, I liked to watch her when she rolled out the dough. She would say it had to be so thin you can see though it.

Strudel has become a family tradition. Now our son is peeling and slicing the apples, and his wife does the rest. Hopefully, our granddaughter will carry on the tradition.

MARTHA GREENEMEIER

The entire Greenemeier family held a picnic every year around Father's Day. *Kraut Kuche*, or cabbage buns, were our traditional picnic food for many years. They are a delicious all-in-one-meal that is eaten hot, but held like a sandwich. All the women in our family got together at Grandma Katherine Greenemeier's house to help put the *Kraut Kuche* together. Grandma started the bread dough and filling ahead of time. We all helped assemble the buns, sometimes making as many as 200 at a time. When they were finally put together, we would each take a pan or two home to be baked in our oven before meeting in Humboldt Park for the picnic. Grandma would make a gallon of tea. Fresh lemons were sliced and brought along. We served Kool-Aid to the children. Grandma didn't supply dessert, so sometimes several of us brought cakes and cookies. Aunt Martha usually brought lots of fresh fruits and goodies for the children. It was such a special day!

KRAUT KUCHE (CABBAGE BUNS)

INGREDIENTS

DOUGH

2 cups warm water
1 pkg. dry yeast
2 Tbsp. sugar
1 Tbsp. salt
5-1/2 to 6 cups all-purpose flour
2 Tbsp. shortening

FILLING

3 lbs. chuck roast, roasted and ground
3 large white onions, coarsely sliced
3 lbs. cabbage, coarsely sliced
2 Tbsp. oil
Salt and black pepper to taste

To make the bread in a large mixing bowl, combine the water, sugar, salt, shortening, and yeast with three cups of flour. Beat vigorously for several minutes. Fold in the remaining flour and let rest for about 5 to 10 minutes. Remove from bowl and place on a lightly floured surface. Knead the dough for 10 minutes, or until it is smooth and elastic. Place the dough in a greased bowl and set aside to allow the dough to rise, doubling its size. For convenience, frozen bread dough can be substituted.

Preheat the oven to 350 degrees. For the filling, add oil to a frying pan, then onions and layer cabbage on top. Cover and sauté until tender, stirring as needed. Bacon fat may be brushed on top if desired. Set the filling aside to cool.

When the bread dough has risen, punch it down and pinch off pieces large enough to roll into four or five inch squares. Put a heaping spoonful of filling into the center of each dough square. Bring the corners together and seal the edges. Place the buns in a greased pan with the sealed edges down. Allow to rise. Bake in a 350 degree oven for 35 to 45 minutes, or until the buns are nicely browned. Each bun is a serving.

SERVES 30 TO 36

PORK RIBS AND SAUERKRAUT

INGREDIENTS

1 1/2 lbs. Sauerkraut
1 1/2 cups chopped yellow onion
1 1/2 lbs. tomatoes, diced
1 cup brown sugar
3 lbs. pork ribs, bone-in

MONIKA OBSTOY

As far back as I can remember, we always had pork ribs and Sauerkraut at special family gatherings. This dish was a natural favorite, since cabbage, onions, and tomatoes were always homegrown. We also had plenty of fresh pork because we raised pigs on our farm in the country. I hope you will enjoy making this tasty dish as much as my family and friends enjoy eating it.

Preheat oven to 325 degrees. Layer the ingredients in a large casserole dish or roasting pan, starting with the Sauerkraut and ending with the ribs. Do not stir. Cover the dish with foil and bake at 325 degrees for three hours. Remove the foil and bake uncovered for the last 45 minutes. Serve with mashed potatoes.

SERVES 6

SPÄTZLE

SUSAN GROSSKOPH

When my Grandmother Kaufman visited us during the holidays, a highlight was watching her cut the Spätzle dough into the boiling water. When the Spätzle rose to the top, I could scoop them up.

Helping her is one of my fondest memories. *Spätzle* is the diminutive form of *Spätz*, or "small sparrows."

INGREDIENTS

3/4 cup all-purpose flour
1 egg
1 egg yolk
1/4 cup milk
1 Tbsp. butter
Salt and black pepper to taste
Breadcrumbs (optional)
2 to 3 slices Swiss cheese (optional)

Combine flour, salt, and black pepper on a large plate. Make a space in the center of the dry ingredients. Add one egg, one additional egg yolk, and the milk to the center of the plate. Beat gently to mix. Gradually stir in the flour mixture to form a thin dough.

Bring a large pot of salted water to a rapid boil. Dip a sharp knife into the water, then slice off small pieces of the dough with the knife from the plate. Be sure to wet the knife every few slices.

Carefully slide the slices into the boiling water.

When the cooked Spätzle float to the surface, remove and drain well. Shown here with chicken and mixed vegetables.

Variation: Place cooked Spätzle in a baking dish with butter and toss to mix. Place Swiss cheese slices over the layer of Spätzle and top with breadcrumbs. Bake at 350 degrees until Swiss cheese melts.

SIDE DISH MAKES 4 SERVINGS

PFLAUMENKUCHEN (PLUM CAKE)

INGREDIENTS

20 to 28 Italian plums,
*   pitted and quartered*
Whipping cream
Sugar

PASTRY

4 cups all-purpose flour
1 cup sugar
3/4 cup unsalted butter,
*   softened*
1 egg
1 tsp. vanilla
2 to 3 tbsp. milk

CUSTARD

4 egg yolks
8 Tbsp. sugar
4 Tbsp. milk

STREUSEL

1-3/4 cups all-purpose flour
1 cup sugar
3/4 cup unsalted butter
1 tsp. lemon peel, grated

TRAUDL MESSER

I remember all the delicious fresh fruit *tortes* and cakes that mothers baked for their families during the summer months when I lived in Germany. We had rhubarb, apple, gooseberry, strawberry, and cherry treats. But, when August and September came, it was *Pflaumenkuchen* (plum cake) time in my hometown of Grimma, located between Leipzig and Dresden, in Saxony.

I first learned how to bake when I came to Milwaukee in 1949. *Pflaumenkuchen* was on the top of my list to learn. When I asked my mother for her recipe, letters began flying back and forth between America and Germany. They were filled with questions from me and answers from her. Finally, after a long search for the right *Pflaumen* (Italian plums), and lots of practice, I mastered my mother's *Pflaumenkuchen*.

Preheat the oven to 400 degrees. Butter and flour two nine-inch cake pans. Combine the flour and sugar in a mixing bowl. Cut the softened butter into the flour mixture. Add the egg, vanilla, and milk to the mixture. Add extra flour if necessary to make the dough smooth. Divide the dough in half and pat on the bottom of the pan forming it 1 inch up the sides of the pan. Arrange the pitted and quartered plum slices on top of the dough.

Combine the custard ingredients in a mixing bowl. Mix well and pour on top of the plums.

Combine the *Streusel* ingredients in a bowl and mix until firm and crumbly. Spread the *Streusel* evenly on top of the cake. Bake for 10 minutes at 400 degrees. Reduce the heat to 375 degrees and bake for an additional 35 to 40 minutes, or until the *Streusel* is golden brown. Remove the pans from the oven and allow them to cool on a rack. When you are ready to serve, slice the cake and remove it from the cake pan. Dust the slices with powdered sugar. I also like to use fresh peaches and other fruits instead of plums. Whip the cream with 2 tablespoons of sugar until soft peaks form. Place in a crystal bowl for serving.

SERVES 8

LEBERKNOEDEL SUPPE
(BEEF LIVER DUMPLING SOUP)

TRUDY PARADIS

A family favorite, this soup is a frequent request for special occasions. An enduring (and funny) family story is that an uncle intensely disliked liver. So his wife, my mother's sister, and the other "cooks" called this soup "Meat Dumplings" and he not only ate them up, but asked for them if he hadn't had them in a while!

Today, we often wait until guests have eaten (and loved) the dumplings before we tell them they're "Liver Dumplings." *Guten Apetit!*

INGREDIENTS

1 1/2 lbs. beef liver, trimmed
1 medium onion
1 bunch parsley, stemmed
3 to 4 cups bread crumbs
5 eggs, beaten
1/2 cup all-purpose flour
Salt, black pepper and nutmeg to taste
1 cube beef bouillon
1 stick butter
Chives for garnish

Grind liver, onion, and parsley together. Combine all ingredients and allow mixture to rest for a few hours.

Boil water in 2 or 3 large pots. Add salt. Drop the dumpling mixture by spoonfuls into boiling water. Cook at a slow boil for 20 to 30 minutes. Add bouillon and melted, browned butter (or chicken or beef stock). Garnish with chives.

Serve and enjoy!

SERVES 6

ROTE GRUETZE (RED PUDDING)

Place all the currants, 2 cups of the raspberries, water and lemon peel into a sauce pan and bring to a boil. Simmer the mixture until the fruit is soft. Allow the mixture to cool slightly and puree the mixture through a food mill.

Return the pureed fruit to the sauce pan. Add sugar and salt and bring back to a boil. More sugar may be needed if fruit is not ripe enough. Mix cornstarch with cold water until it dissolves, then stir slowly into the fruit mixture. Boil for one minute, and then remove the pan from the heat. Stir in the lemon juice and the remaining two cups of raspberries. As the mixture cools, pour it into a serving dish, or individual dishes, and chill for several hours.

Serve this dish with a custard sauce or whipped cream.

Try the dish using blueberries and blackberries for a *Blaue Gruetze*.

SERVES 6 TO 8

INGREDIENTS

4 cups red currants
4 cups red raspberries
2 cups water
2 small pieces lemon peel
1 cup sugar
1 pinch of salt
1 cup cornstarch
1 tsp. lemon juice

VALERIE BRUMDER

The Germans are always thrilled when fresh fruit is in season; they continually look for new ways to serve it.

One of the popular recipes for berries is *Rote Gruetze*. This name may be hard to pronounce, but it sounds much more sophisticated than its simple English translation: Red Pudding.

The dessert is versatile, so it can be made with any red fruit. My favorite combination is currants and raspberries.

GRETCHEN TITUS

This recipe, which my family calls "Arta's Ham Loaves," is from my great aunt Martha Bowman. She was very talented and painted the Rosenthal china shown in the picture. My original copy of this recipe is in a letter dated February 1952 to one of her sisters. She says, "…half of the recipe is enough for four women — men might prefer more." My cousins have adapted the recipe to make meat balls. They serve them in a chafing dish as appetizers.

ARTA'S HAM LOAVES

INGREDIENTS

LOAVES
1 lb. ham, ground
1 lb. pork, ground
2 cups soft bread crumbs
2 eggs, beaten
1 cup milk
1 small onion, chopped
1/8 tsp. pepper

SAUCE
1/2 cup vinegar
1/2 cup water
1/2 cup brown sugar
1 tsp. dry mustard

Combine the eggs, milk, and breadcrumbs in a large bowl. With hands, mix in the ground ham and ground pork. Form the meat into small oblong loaves. Preheat the oven to 275 degrees. To make the sauce, bring the sauce ingredients to a boil.

Pour the sauce over the ham loaves. Bake covered for 1 to 2 hours at 275 degrees. During the last 20 minutes of cooking, remove the cover to allow the ham loaves to lightly brown.

SERVES 6 TO 12

PFLAUMEN KNOEDEL (PLUM DUMPLINGS)

The night before you plan to serve *Pflaumen Knoedel*, peel and boil the potatoes. When the potatoes are done, drain the water and let them cool to room temperature before ricing. Place in a large bowl and set aside. In preparation for making this dish, you should also freeze the Italian plums the night before. Freezing "juices" them. Thaw and use in the recipe.

Cream two tablespoons of butter and beat in the eggs and salt. Gradually beat in the flour and potatoes. The dough should be somewhat stiff. Don't handle it too much.

On a floured board, roll out the dough to a 1/4 inch thickness, and cut into three-inch squares. Cut each plum open on one side, leaving the pit in. Place one whole plum on each square, and sprinkle with a heaping teaspoon of cinnamon sugar. Fold the edges over the plum and shape into a ball with hands. The dough should form a thin layer around the plum.

Gently lower dumplings into the boiling water and allow to simmer for 15 minutes. The dumplings are ready when they float to the top. Carefully remove with a slotted spoon. Drain briefly, then roll the dumplings in buttered bread crumbs to coat. Keep the dumplings warm in the oven until ready to serve. Generously sprinkle more buttered bread-crumbs on top. If desired, sprinkle additional cinnamon sugar.

When served, cut open the dumplings, and lay the pit on the side of your plate. Tradition says each person keeps "count" of how many dumplings were eaten.

CARLA DUMKE

My grandmother, Nala, brought this recipe with her from Bergreichenstein, Bohemia to America in 1906. This area, currently part of the Czech Republic, was close to the current German border and has been part of many countries over the years.

My mother, a great cook, took this family recipe for *Pflaumen Knoedel* from Oma Nala to continue the tradition in America. When my uncles would visit, my mother proudly made the family's famous plum dumplings. There were never any leftovers. The farm boys would stuff themselves, competing amongst each other to see who would have the most pits on the side of his plate.

My family continues to celebrate each September with our own Plum Dumpling Fest.

INGREDIENTS

2 *eggs*
2 *cups sifted all-purpose unbleached flour*
1 *cup fine bread crumbs, mixed with melted butter*
12-15 *Italian plums or apricots*
6 *med. boiled Idaho potatoes, riced*
1/3 *cup cinnamon sugar*
1 1/2 *tsp. salt*
butter

BLITZ TORTE

ROBIN PARADIS-KENT

The *Blitz Torte* was my Oma's favorite and best "party" dessert. We asked for it for birthdays and looked forward to it on holidays, when friends and family visited. Today, when I make it, friends "ooh" and "ahh" because it looks so scrumptious and tastes even better when Rachel and I make it.

INGREDIENTS

1 cup sifted cake flour
2 tsp. baking powder
1/4 tsp. salt
1/2 cup soft shortening or butter
1-1/2 cups sugar
4 eggs, separated
2 tsp. vanilla
1/3 cup milk
1/2 cup finely chopped nuts
1/2 pint whipping cream
2 tbsp. powdered sugar
1 small pkg. vanilla pudding

Prepare your favorite custard recipe or an instant packaged vanilla pudding mix ahead of time (small box to serve four). Chill overnight.

Have the shortening or butter, and eggs at room temperature. Preheat the oven to 350 degrees. Grease two eight-inch cake pans, sprinkling with all-purpose flour, and shaking out the excess. Sift cake flour once before measuring. Separate eggs. Chop or grind almonds, pecans, hazelnuts or walnuts to equal 1/2 cup.

Sift together cake flour, baking powder, and salt, then set aside this sifted mixture.

In a large mixing bowl, add softened shortening or butter, sugar, unbeaten egg yolks, and vanilla. Beat this mixture, scraping the bowl often. Slowly add the sifted flour mixture and milk. Beat this until it is well blended. Pour batter into prepared cake pans, distributing evenly.

Wash and thoroughly dry beaters. In a small mixing bowl, beat egg whites until soft peaks form, then add sugar and vanilla and continue beating until blended.

Spread the egg white mixture over the top of the cake batter in pans. Slightly push the batter up onto the sides of the pans. Sprinkle with chopped nuts. Bake at 350 degrees for about 40 minutes. Carefully remove the cakes from pans and allow to cool on wire racks. With thoroughly cleaned beaters, whip cream into soft peaks and add powdered sugar. Continue whipping until stiff peaks are formed.

Place one layer of the cake, meringue side down, on a serving plate. Spread the chilled custard or pudding mix over this layer, then place the second layer, meringue side up. Spread the whipped cream and decorate with sliced or whole strawberries, or other fruit.

SERVES 8-12

HASELNUSS KUCHEN
(HAZELNUT CAKE)

INGREDIENTS

1 lb. hazelnuts, ground
8 oz. sugar
4 1/8 tsp. baking powder
2 tsp. rum extract
8 eggs
3 to 4 oz. marzipan

MARIANNE STUMBAUGH

In Germany it is custom to serve *Kaffe* and *Kuchen*, or coffee and cake, on Sundays. This practice is similar to the English custom of serving afternoon tea to guests.

As far back as I can remember, my mother baked a cake every Sunday afternoon. Her hazelnut cake used to be my favorite. When I left Germany as a young girl, I had never learned to bake since my mother worked during the week. I was delighted to learn that my brother Manfred had preserved my mother's recipe. The last time he was here for a visit, he showed me how to bake a hazelnut cake. I was able to serve it to my family on Sundays, just as my mother had done in Germany.

Preheat the oven to 415 degrees. Combine the nuts, sugar, and baking powder in a large bowl, mixing well. Add the rum extract. In a separate bowl, beat the eggs till foamy. Incorporate the eggs into the nut mixture. Pour the batter into a well greased springform 9 inch pan. Put the rolled marzipan around in a circle and press into the batter. Cover the pan with foil and bake at 425 degrees for 45 minutes. Remove the foil, and continue baking for 15 minutes. The hazelnut cake tastes best when served with whipped cream.

SERVES 10-12

HOTELS

Early travelers, wanderers, visitors – anyone requiring shelter – slept wherever they could lay down their heads, including in lean-tos, barns, and spare rooms. To meet the need, and for additional income, families who had any extra space rented beds and fed their boarders. Those with larger houses or several spare rooms operated as rooming houses, while others built hotels to accommodate the need for sleeping and eating on a fancier (and more expensive) scale.

In 1862, Christian Fernekes & Bros. managed the St. Charles Hotel on Market Square. It had all the modern conveniences of the time: steam heat, elevator, water power, parlors, sample rooms, and more.

Guido Pfister's dream was realized when he began building the "Grand Hotel of the West." However, though he never saw it finished, his son oversaw the completion of the Pfister Hotel, an 1890s Romanesque masterpiece in downtown Milwaukee. "The Jewel of Milwaukee" has the largest collection of nineteenth century Victorian art on display of any hotel in the world. Originally known as the "Astor-on-the-Lake," the Astor Hotel, (built by real estate developer Oscar Brachman for Milwaukee hotel tycoon Walter Schroeder), was completed in 1920, and was considered one of the finest hotels in the Midwest. In 1984, the Astor Hotel was added to the National Register of Historic Places.

Other hotels from early Milwaukee have been remodeled into apartments, rooming houses and condominiums, while still others, sadly, have been demolished.

The Blatz Hotel and Café is pictured on the left of the photo. In the center behind the trolley is the Pabst Theater. The statue of Henry Bergh, the founder of The Society for the Prevention of Cruelty to Animals, with the horse watering trough, is in the left foreground. The only building remaining today in City Hall Square is the Pabst Theater.

The Schlitz Hotel was built in 1887. The hotel was lighted with electricity throughout, a step-up in luxury. The arched entrance on the right leads into the Schlitz Palm Garden. Cream City brick was used here, as it was on many buildings in Milwaukee. When local clay is fired, the resulting color is an unusual pale yellow. Although the percentage of iron remains the same as in other brick, the high percentage of calcium and magnesium overrides the red iron color.

Visiting dignitaries, professional sports teams, musicians, and other stars stay at the Pfister Hotel. The first important dignitary to celebrate there was Crown Prince Heinrich of Prussia in 1893.

Alvin P. Kletzch

The Republican House Hotel was a grand building located at the corner of Old World Third Street and Kilbourn Avenue. Charles Kletsch made this friendly downtown hotel a success. Later, his son, Alvin, managed the hotel. It is the birthplace of the American Legion. Kletsch Park, on the Milwaukee River in Glendale (a near-north suburb of Milwaukee) is named for their family. In 1935, Milwaukee Chess Club rented rooms and kept them open around the clock for members to play chess.

This Art-Deco-style Schroeder Hotel was built in 1928, by Walter Schroeder, on the site of the Potawatomi Indian Village. He built hotels in four Midwestern states, but the Schroeder was his largest. Currently named the Hilton Milwaukee City Center, it retains its opulent marble lobby and majestic ballrooms.

HOMES

German-speaking settlements developed in the city hall area because it was a vacant, lowland marsh. The more affluent, English-speaking Yankees settled up on the hills east of the Milwaukee River. The main shopping street in the German neighborhood of the 1880s developed on the west side of this river, on Third Street. As the population grew, the German neighborhoods spread north and west from downtown. Stretching to the west from downtown, Grand Avenue showcased many homes of wealthy German families. Later, Highland Boulevard, with its grand homes, became known as Sauerkraut Boulevard. After 1900, many financially established German families began moving to the East Side along Lake Michigan's bluffs.

Streets were named for the famous and the important. Beethoven Place was named by Milwaukee Germans who formed the Beethoven Society in 1843. Meinecke Avenue was named for the toy manufacturer; Miller Lane, for the brewery owner Fred Miller; Messmer Street and High School for the Archbishop of Milwaukee in 1903. Bettinger Place is named for Nicholas Bettinger and his relatives. He emigrated from Prussia to Buffalo, New York, in 1840. In 1841, he and his five cousins literally walked to Milwaukee. This group of cousins embodied varied occupations such as trapper, hunter, bricklayer, and tavern owner. His son became owner of a hotel and saloon.

Auer, Becher, Fiebrantz, Pabst (which became Lloyd Street), Rohr, and Schiller are just some of the many German-inspired street names found in Milwaukee today.

Some streets and areas were named for German cities, like New Coeln (Köln) and Bremen. Others were named for trees brought from their homeland – Linden.

Alexander Humboldt (1769-1859) was a German explorer, naturalist, scientist – probably the most famous man in Europe (aside from Napoleon) in the first half of the 19th Century. Even though Humboldt never lived in Milwaukee, there is an avenue, boulevard, court, and even a park named after him!

Businesses and workers' homes often stood nestled together. Thus, no transportation was needed as people could walk to and from work easily.

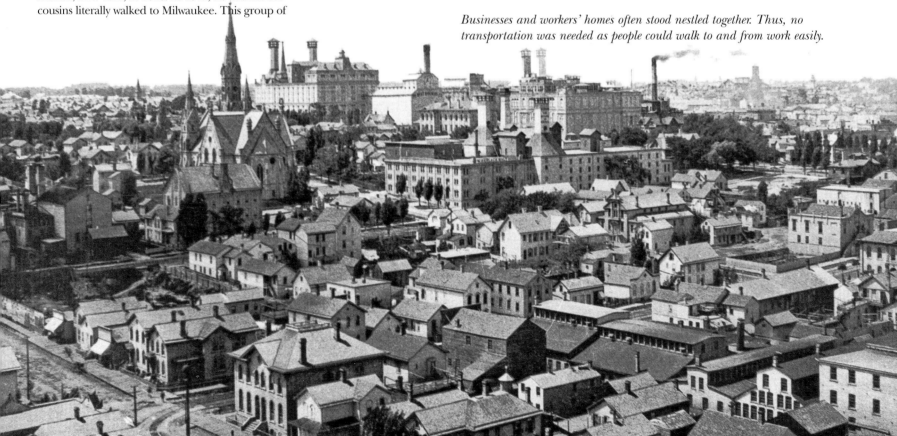

Originally constructed for beer baron
Frederick Pabst, this home was
designed by Ferry & Clas between
1890-1893. The conservatory,
designed by Otto Strack, was originally
an exhibit pavilion for the display of
Pabst products at the 1893 Columbian
Exposition in Chicago. In 1906, the
mansion became the residence of
Archbishop Messmer. In 1976, it was
sold, and because it was destined to
become a parking lot, preservation-
minded citizens rallied and saved the
splendid building, which is now
restored and welcomes visitors throughout the year.

The impressive Schlesinger-Gallun mansion was on Prospect Avenue.

*This residence on Lake Drive was built by tanner Fred Vogel, Jr. It has 23 rooms,
ten fireplaces, and a wide view of Lake Michigan.*

The Mitchell House Gazebo, with etched glass, is one of the finest surviving gazebos in the country. Built for viewing the surrounding gardens and greenhouse, the restored one-and-a-half story, wooden structure remains just as impressive now as it was then.

Built in 1855, the resplendent Alexander Mitchell mansion was remodeled in 1870. "In a symbolic act of ethnic ascendancy, the Deutscher Club took over Alexander Mitchell's mansion after the Scottish tycoon's death and made it a leading center of Gemütlichkeit." Today Milwaukeeans know it as the Wisconsin Club on Wisconsin Avenue.

On Kilbourn Avenue, the Kalvelage Mansion (above) is known as a Baroque gem of historical and architectural significance. Built in 1898 by architect Otto Strack for plumbing supply magnate Joseph Kalvelage, (the son of a German immigrant who was a soap maker), and decorated by Cyril Colnik, ("the Tiffany of Iron Work Craftsmen"), the mansion was most recently a museum of mechanical instruments and is now a private home again.

Grain broker Robert Nunnemacher built this mansion on a triple lot on Wahl Avenue. Wahl Avenue skirts Lake Park and is named after the "Father of Milwaukee Parks," Christian Wahl. Alexander C. Eschweiler, a prominent local architect, designed this home.

The magnificent Blatz Family home was located on Van Buren Street, whereas many of the other prominent brewers had homes on Highland Avenue. It was a three-story building which had running hot and cold water, marble washbasins, and a marble fireplace – all exceptional innovations for the 1880s.

The founders of the Ambrosia factory, the Schoenlebers, lived in this 1890s side-by-side home. Daughters Marie L. and Louise Schoenleber donated a clocktower to the city in memory of their parents. It was placed in front of the Milwaukee County Courthouse, the former site of the first Ambrosia plant, but it was eventually moved elsewhere.

Milwaukee Architects

Eugene Liebert

Liebert left a notable architectural legacy in Milwaukee. Perhaps the best known of his commercial work is the Germania Building. He also designed churches for Catholics and Lutherans alike, and his many commissions included the Harnischfeger, Bergenthal and Trostel mansions and the South Side Natatorium. Six of his buildings are on the National Register of Historic Places.

Erhard Brielmaier

Both the Gothic Revival style gate house and Romanesque chapel at the Calvary Cemetery were designed by architect Erhard Brielmaier, who also designed the Basilica of St. Josaphat on Milwaukee's South Side.

Milwaukee Public Library and Museum Building, as seen here in 1895, was built by the Ferry & Clas Architectural Firm.

Alexander C. Eschweiler

Eschweiler was one of the most commercially successful architects in the Milwaukee area; designing schools, churches, office buildings, and private residences. He also designed the Charles Allis Art Library, the Milwaukee-Downer "Quad," the West Allis Wadham's Gas Station, and the five buildings comprising the Milwaukee County School of Agriculture and Domestic Economy, which is now an Historic District.

Frederick Velguth

Trinity Evangelical Lutheran Church was designed by architect Frederick Velguth in 1878 using Cream City brick. It features a landmark 200-foot spire and sandstone details on the façade. Inside is a magnificent 1,600-pipe organ. Some of his other enduring buildings can be seen today on Old World Third Street.

TRANSPORTATION

In villages and towns, people could walk wherever they needed to go. Everything they needed was nearby: their work, the baker, the butcher, the *Gasthaus* (inn), the town hall, the church, the tavern – all were within a stroll's distance. As these villages and towns grew, transportation became necessary. Some people did not earn enough to be able to stable horses or later buy cars while living in the city. As such, they depended on public transportation to get them to and from work, church, the grocer, and entertainment.

Early public transportation on the Greenfield Line shows two horses pulling a trolley. Adults paid a nickel for a ride with transfer privileges, from 9 am to 11 pm.

The electric streetcar traveled over the Wells Street viaduct, across the Menomonee Valley in 1904. Good old Number 10!

Milwaukee grew into a city, which required mass transit. As early as 1860 there was a *Pferdebahn* (horse-drawn trolley); by 1890 there were electric streetcars; and by 1900, there were 13 different streetcar lines and a rapid transit system called the Milwaukee Electric Railway and Light Company, which went to Port Washington, Burlington, and East Troy. This interurban system allowed people living in outlying areas to commute to work and enjoy the city's cultural offerings, sports, restaurants, and other entertainment. It also allowed the city dwellers to travel to neighboring towns and villages to visit friends, relatives, and other attractions. By 1903, ninety-eight percent of urban transit was electrified.

By 1936, rubber-tired buses joined the trolley cars as alternate means of transportation. As a result, the city gradually removed the tracks from the streets, and in 1958, Milwaukee saw the end of streetcars.

These Milwaukeeans are waiting for the trolley which will take them to Captain Hintz's Resort at Belleview Beach on Pewaukee Lake.

This is the Frederick Renta Saloon, circa 1900, on 12th Street. The trolley out front is headed for Schlitz Park where many families spent their free time. Also, three horse-drawn lines took people to various parks and summer gardens.

Electric cars began appearing on Milwaukee's streets in 1890.

*Cars line a bustling city street as the trolleys navigate their way through town
on 3rd Street between State Street and Highland Avenue, circa 1930s.*

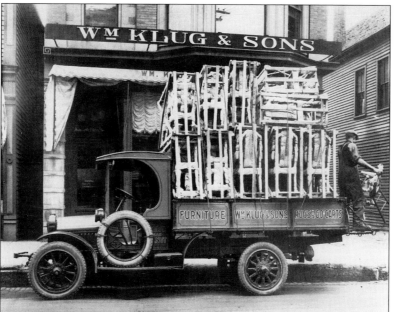

Transporting people and things required different vehicles. Although it would seem the cargo is stacked precariously, we can hope this delivery arrived with everything intact.

Bendfeldt's Ice Cream was a very popular treat – advertised here on a very snazzy delivery vehicle.

Kuhl Motors was a large Ford dealership downtown. In the background are the Milwaukee Civic Auditorium and the newly constructed Sports Arena. In the far distance to the right is City Hall.

Early trains carried freight (grain and other goods) beginning in 1847, when the Milwaukee and Waukesha Railroad first appeared. The railroad then enlarged to cross the state as the Milwaukee and Mississippi Railroad. As the rails were extended, passengers began to ride the trains, starting in 1851, on a six-mile line running from Milwaukee to Wauwatosa, Wisconsin.

The Milwaukee Road (officially the Chicago, Milwaukee, St. Paul and Pacific Railroad) operated in the Midwest and Northwest from 1847 until it was acquired by and merged with the Soo Line Railway in 1985. The 1890s Chicago and Milwaukee Electric Railroad was renamed in 1916 to the Chicago North Shore and Milwaukee Railroad.

Mayor Carl Zeidler cuts the ribbon at Milwaukee Terminal to inaugurate North Shore Line's Electroliner on February 6, 1941. A ride on board would mean a clean, safe trip from Milwaukee to Chicago in only 90 minutes.

The Milwaukee Road (officially the Chicago, Milwaukee, St. Paul and Pacific Railroad) Depot in the heart of downtown Milwaukee was in a desirable location for access to hotels, businesses, and entertainment establishments. From it, the streamlined Hiawatha, *a favorite among railroad fans, made daily trips to the West.*

At the lakefront station of the Chicago Northwestern Railroad, both freight and passengers, in great numbers, were transported to and from Milwaukee. The depot was demolished in the 1960s, and the resulting outcry started a preservation movement in Milwaukee.

GERMAN MONUMENTS

Johann Wolfgang von Goethe (1749-1832) and Friedrich von Schiller (1759-1805) were great German poets, dramatists, and writers whose works and lives have influenced liberal German thinkers for the past two centuries. Within German immigrant communities in the United States, it became common to form associations based on one's home region in Germany. In Milwaukee, there was a strong Schwaben Benevolent Aid Society, which was especially proud of their fellow Schwab, Schiller. Then, the Schwaben began a movement to erect a statue to Schiller in Milwaukee, but soon other German societies in Milwaukee wanted to participate.

Subsequently, a coalition of thirty German organizations and prominent German families raised funds for a monument in honor of Schiller and Goethe. The bronze statue was created by Ernest Rietschel and was cast in the early 1900s from the original model of 1847. It stands today in Washington Park, near the Blatz Temple of Music. Friedrich Heine, chief artist of the Panorama artists of Milwaukee, designed the granite pedestal on which the Goethe-Schiller Monument stands.

Coincidentally, Rietschel also cast a smaller ten-foot version of the original bronze statue of the Germania, which today stands on a hilltop called Niederwald, overlooking the Rhine River near Koblenz, Germany. The Milwaukee statue was installed on the Germania building in 1908, and was removed in 1917.

Henry Bergh (1811-1888), the founder of the American Society for the Prevention of Cruelty to Animals, was a descendant of the Bergh family of the Rhineland in Germany. A bronze statue of Bergh was originally erected atop an animal watering trough in Market Square, the site of a German Farmers' Market. When the present Milwaukee City Hall was built on Market Square in 1895, there were few horses requiring the water trough. Therefore, the water trough was replaced with a flower bed, on which the statue stood.

In 1908, this monument in Washington Park was dedicated to the great poets Goethe and Schiller, both well-respected philosophers and dramatists. It is the only monument dedicated to both of them in the United States.

This statue of Henry Bergh was placed in Market Square in 1891. The hotel in the background, formerly the Pabst Hotel, then the St. James Hotel, no longer exists. Bergh, a philanthropist, was the founder of the American Society for the Prevention of Cruelty to Animals. In 1966, the statue was moved to the Wisconsin Humane Society on North Humboldt Avenue, and now the statue of Bergh petting a dog is at the current Humane Society site on West Wisconsin Avenue.

King Gambrinus represents the legendary First Brewer of Beer. In 1857, a statue of King Gambrinus was placed at the Pabst Brewing Company. Originally carved of wood, deterioration necessitated its replacement by an aluminum version in 1967. In the mid-1970s, Sid Stone (an immigrant artist from Berlin, Germany) purchased and moved the statue to Stonecroft, a mock-European village 20 miles north of Milwaukee, where it was later struck by lightning and perished.

Baron Friedrich Wilhelm von Steuben, an aristocrat and Prussian Army officer, came to America in 1777, and volunteered his military talents to General George Washington at Valley Forge. He trained the inexperienced soldiers of the Continental Army into a competent military force. The Milwaukee branch of the Steuben Society, an English-speaking organization founded in St. Louis in 1919, commissioned the monument of the German-born hero. Dedicated in 1921, it was placed outside of Washington Park at West Lisbon Avenue, Lloyd Street and North Sherman Boulevard.

TURNERS

Turnen in German means to do gymnastics. Frederick Ludwig Jahn introduced exercise to the students at the University of Berlin in 1811. Being the first to conceptualize the idea of combining athletics with scholarship, Jahn hoped to strengthen his students, in mind and body, so that they might one day overthrow Napoleon and his occupying armies. The first Turner instructors came to America from Germany to teach at Amherst College and at Harvard. After the failed 1848 revolutions in Germany, many more Turners followed.

American Turner principles, briefly summarized, are as follows: liberty, against all oppression; tolerance, against all fanaticism; reason, against all superstition; justice, against all exploitation; free speech; free press; and free assembly for the discussion of all questions, so that men and women may think unfettered and order their lives by the dictates of conscience. Such is their ideal, which they strive to attain through "A Sound Mind in a Sound Body," the Turner motto. Hundreds of *Turnverein* were established in America, especially in Midwestern towns. In Milwaukee, the West Side Turners organized in 1853. There were other Turner organizations in the city, but the Milwaukee West Side Turners is still in existence today, known as the Milwaukee Turners on Fourth Street.

After the Civil War, Turner George Brosius returned to Milwaukee to be the first paid Turner instructor in the city. One of his graduates went on to reorganize West Point's exercise program. Moreover, the Turner-founded *Turnlehrer Schule* (gymnastics teachers' school), which trained teachers, relocated to the German-English Academy

The Turnverein Building on Fourth Street.

This facility is still used for such Turner activities as gymnastics for children, fencing, a climbing wall, and ladies' exercise classes.

building east of the Milwaukee River and then, at the turn of the 20th century, to the University of Indiana.

The present *Turnhall* (Turner building) is a National Historic Landmark. It houses the same programs and art works that other Turner organizations may have, but the Milwaukee members' involvement in establishing the Social Democratic Party in America sets it apart from the other *Turnhalls* in the country. The 1883 structure is the last vestige of 19th century German Milwaukee standing downtown that is still devoted to its original purpose. The restaurant continues to be open to the public. In addition to the on-going gymnastics program, the Turners produce and record, at the *Turnhall* site, the 4th Street Forum, a public television panel show in which qualified guests discuss relevant issues of the day with input from an audience of interested citizens.

This is an example of a group gymnastics display in the Turner Gymnasium.

Pictured here are athletes holding Indian Clubs, a sort of elongated bowling pin which was used in a rhythmic gymnastic exercise.

The Frankfurter Riege (team) of 1880 posed with instructor George Brosius, holding their special trophy.

The current downtown Milwaukee Turners began as the West Side Turnverein (Gymnastics Club) in 1853. Throughout the city, other Turner organizations included South Side Turners (1868), North Side Turners (1869), Turnverein Vorwärts (1879), Turnverein Bahn Frei (1891), Humboldt Turnverein (1891). Each of these had a training school for adults and children, supervised by experienced instructors.

Turnverein Bahn Frei

Milwaukee restaurateur, R. C. Schmidt, currently operates the Historic Turner Restaurant in the Turner building. Schmidt utilized historic Turner and Milwaukee photographs and memorabilia to create a warm, inviting atmosphere. The popular establishment has one room that features the decor of the old Schlitz Palm Garden restaurant. In 2006, an elevator was added for access to the restaurant and ballroom, which are both undergoing renovation.

Christopher Bach's Orchestra performed for a May Day party in 1926. On Sunday afternoons, in the Milwaukee Turners' ballroom, families met to socialize, drink coffee, eat cakes, sip wine, smoke cigars, and often to watch gymnastic exhibitions moved up from the gym. There were also games for children.

Mach schnell .....

SPORTS

Prior to leaving their native German realms, many would-be immigrants frequently enjoyed participating in a wide variety of sports. In fact, many played on formally organized teams. Yet, when the early German immigrants arrived, no such organized sports activities existed. However, this void was quickly filled by eager athletes looking to engage in their favorite sports.

Both participation and spectator sports lured Germans with their passion for *frische Luft* (fresh air) and *zum Freien* (outdoors). *Einen Spaziergang machen* (to take a walk) was probably the most common activity. Children's backyard games eventually led to more formalized sports involvements, the most prevalent being *Fussball* (soccer), which children played on the street, in the schoolyards, and in fields; while men played in stadiums, both semi-pro and professional. The *Fussball* clubs of this time laid the foundation for the popularity of soccer today.

Aside from walking, women most frequently played the game of *Faustball* (fistball), much like volleyball.

Milwaukee's proximity to Lake Michigan, to many small lakes and to the city rivers afforded convenient access for water sports of all kinds. *Schwimmen* (swimming), *Rudern* (rowing), *Regatta* (racing), and *Segeln* (sailing) were extremely popular in fair weather.

Frozen waters and snow presented another set of sports possibilities, including *Schlittschuhlaufen* (ice skating), *Skilaufen* (skiing), and *Stock Schiessball* (a version of ice hockey).

In addition, many other sports were conducted inside, such as *Kegeln* (bowling), *Turnen* (gymnastics), *Fechten* (fencing), *Boxen* (boxing) and *Ringkampfen* (wrestling).

Among the many organizations which promoted participation in both individual and team sporting activities were Der Deutscher Athletic Club (The German Athletic Club), Der Deutscher Schützen Club (The German Sharpshooting Club), and the *Turnen Gesellschaften* (gymnastics organizations). It has been recognized that Germans, as a group, are not sedentary, and when not actively involved in sports, they seem to enjoy viewing and supporting them.

At an outdoor track, motorbikes raced an oval track.

The Six-Day Bicycle Races are "an almost forgotten sport. During the period from 1890 until 1935, six-day bicycle racing was America's most popular spectator sport." The Milwaukee Wheelmen Club encouraged cycling and held races with prizes.

Recreational target shooting was a popular sport in the middle 1800s. These German sharpshooters of the Schützen Gesellschaft in 1865, practiced their aim and accuracy at Schützen Park [North 3rd and North 5th streets], which became Pabst Park (later Garfield Park, now Rose Park) in Milwaukee.

..... Hurry up

This group photo (1936) was of the **Schwaben Verein für Rasenspiele** *(literally, Club for Outdoor Games on the Green). The men played soccer, the women played fist ball, and boys and girls did gymnastics.*

The Milwaukee Turner Ladies performed gymnastics and continue to do so today. Even though modern gymnasts wear tight leotards, when the current Milwaukee Turner Ladies perform a reenactment, they wear costumes similar to these pictured.

A popular German sport, soccer was transplanted along with immigrants. Soccer teams played on Sundays against other ethnic teams in the city. Families would go to watch the games, picnic, and socialize. Kids would make noises at the opposing goal to distract the players from scoring, just as fans do at today's sporting events.

Later, in the 1900s, Wurftaubenschiessen (trapshooting) became a very popular sport. This gun club, at left, met on the lakefront.

The Inland Lakes Yachting Association supports weekly racing and once a year brings sailors from small midwestern lakes together for a championship regatta. Lake Michigan water can be cold for swimming but residents often charter fishing or sailboat racing. Two important races are the Queen's Cup from Milwaukee to Grand Haven, Michigan and the Mackinac Race, which brings participants from across the country and around the world to compete in the challenging fresh water and sometimes fickle breezes of the Great Lakes. Over the years, the race has become an icon of sailing in the Great Lakes.

Borchert Field (1887-1952), home of the minor league Milwaukee Brewers, was named in 1919 for Otto Borchert, son of a pioneer brewing family. It was a rectangular block, bounded by North 7th and 8th streets and Chambers and Burleigh. It was buried under I-43, Milwaukee's north-south freeway. In 1912 and 1914, the minor league Milwaukee Brewers won the American Association Pennant. In 1920, while playing for the American Association Brewers in his hometown of Milwaukee, Joe Hauser acquired the moniker that would stay with him throughout his career: "Unser Choe" (our Joe). The first baseball game to be played at night under electric lights in Milwaukee was played on June 6, 1935. (A philanthropic family, the Borcherts also donated the lion house at the Milwaukee County Zoo.)

PUBLIC PARKS

Christian Wahl, born in 1829 in Pirmasens, Bavaria, became known as the "Father of the Milwaukee Park System."

Christian had an adventurer's soul, and as such, as a young man he set out to see the world. He went to the gold fields of California and Australia, escaped smallpox in Peru, and walked across the isthmus of Panama. On the ships, he worked his way as a carpenter and common sailor.

Upon returning to America, Wahl settled in Chicago, where he and his brother ran a very large and successful glue manufacturing company, which they sold to meat packer Phillip Armour. In 1886, they returned to Milwaukee as wealthy gentlemen. A public-spirited and progressive citizen, Christian Wahl oversaw the development of Washington, Mitchell, and Lake Parks. Frederick Law Olmstead designed Milwaukee's circle of parks connected by boulevards (linear parks) in conjunction with the Park Commission in 1893.

Christian Wahl utilized his superb taste and wide knowledge of landscape gardening while personally overseeing the transformation of farmland to green breathing space for citizens. After his death, a commemorative sculpture was placed with ceremony at the Lake Park Pavilion.

Some existing Milwaukee County Parks named for Germans include Bender, Boerner, Falk, Froeming, Grobschmidt, Kern, Kletzsch, Lindbergh, Tiefenthaler, Trimborn, Vogel, Wahl, Wehr, and Zeidler.

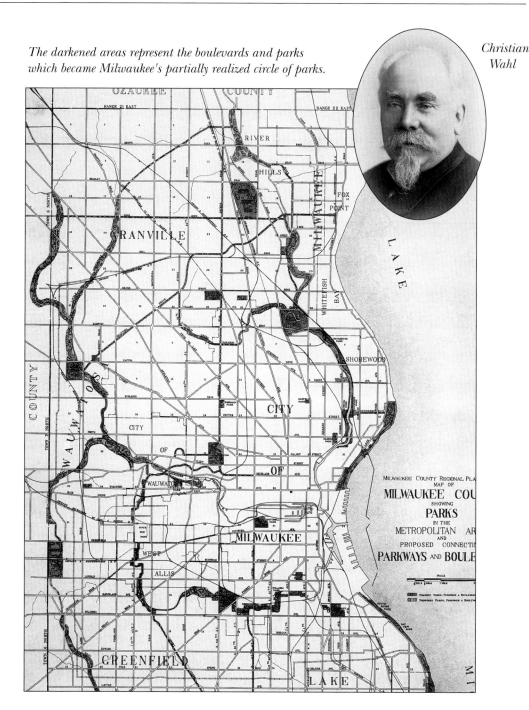

The darkened areas represent the boulevards and parks which became Milwaukee's partially realized circle of parks.

Christian Wahl

Mach schnell.....

RECREATION CENTERS

As Milwaukee developed, sports and recreation were important to both the individual and the employer. Large companies built private parks and made land available to their employees for health and recreation. Healthy employees were happier and more efficient. The breweries developed parks where families could – and did – spend Sunday afternoons having a good time. These venues offered amusements, such as Ferris wheels, carousels, carnival rides, dance pavilions, bandshells, and orchestras. These parks had the spirit of an extended picnic or family reunion where employees not only brought relatives but met co-workers and friends, who became like extended family.

The three major breweries built the largest of these recreational parks. Schlitz built the Schützen Park in Milwaukee; Pabst operated the Whitefish Bay Resort on Lake Michigan; and the Blatz Park, originally the Pleasant Valley Park, was on the Milwaukee River. These private parks later became real-estate developments.

Currently, Milwaukee has a number of nature centers, including Wehr Nature and the Schlitz Audubon Centers. The Wehr is the only nature center located in the southern half of Milwaukee County. The Schlitz parcel of land, situated on what was known as the Nine-Mile Farm, is found along the Lake Michigan shore. Originally owned by the Uihlein Family, it was a horse farm, where the brewery's horses were kept.

Admission tickets

Located on the river, Blatz Park Pavilion was originally the Pleasant Valley Park. People went boating and canoeing, enjoying the fresh air and scenery the river provided. People without their own transportation reached the Pavilion by streetcar or boat. Near the river, a wooded grove stood behind the Pavilion, allowing for leisurely walks and picnics.

Children would stand under-
neath the gazebo and pretend
to direct while musicians
played for the crowd.

These three photos are of Pabst's Whitefish Bay Resort
which was located on Lake Michigan. With a shooting gallery, Ferris wheel, and excellent food and
drink, the Whitefish Bay Resort seemed to have it all.

Between 1889-1914, outdoor movies were shown; the
projector was hand cranked. Visitors arrived either by
carriage, the Whitefish Bay "dummy line" railroad,
or by excursion steamboats from downtown.

Schlitz Park on Eighth and Walnut streets was considered a favorite drinking spot. A schooner of beer was sold for a nickel. Crowds came to hear presidents speak at political rallies, as well as to listen to concerts, including performances by the much-loved Christian Bach. The park was an integral part of city life.

At every party or wedding in the park, and after every concert – everyone danced – no matter if the band or orchestra was large or small. The Waltz, of course, was the big favorite, but the Polka and Schottish were popular, too. Then, when it was time for the Broom Dance (a mixer), there was the hopeful chance that a special person would become your partner.

Electric lights were added to Schlitz Park as early as 1881. The Park, which was considered one of the most beautiful in Milwaukee, had a pagoda, three-story tower, magnificent fountains, concert hall, and restaurant.

SWIM CLUBS

Of the many sports Milwaukee families enjoyed, swimming was probably the most popular. The beach at Lake Michigan was for wading, splashing, sunbathing, playing in the sand and cooling off on hot days, but the Milwaukee River was especially for swimming. Kids of all ages learned to swim at special swimming schools. Then there were races, water polo, and bathing suit contests. Parks along the river offered picnic places, refreshments, amusements, carnival rides, while swim clubs were organized for family activities.

Many children learned to swim at Rohn's Swimming School, one of three schools on the west bank of the Milwaukee River, just north of the North Avenue Dam. Swimming instruction at the time allowed for the instructor to remain on a dock and use a pole to help the child learn to swim. The pole was attached to a rope, which was tied around the swimmer. This enabled the instructor to guide the child through the water.

Some German Milwaukee children spent their summer days playing in the water at the Milwaukee River waterfall at the Carl Schurz Park in Grafton.

Marathon Swimming Races in the Milwaukee River were popular. This group, from Rohn's Swimming School, is an example of both the typical swimming team and the swimming suit styles of 1914.

This 1897 postcard of Bechstein's Swimming School shows a slide, rowboats and canoes. Children attended swimming school, not only to learn to swim, but to enjoy the other amusements as well.

Germans enjoyed their frische luft (fresh air) and made sure their children had ample time to play in and out of the water. Some things never change: note the children in the back row making ears on the other children's heads.

GERMAN EDUCATION

The first Catholic school west of the Alleghenies was founded in the basement of old St. Mary's church in downtown Milwaukee by Sister Caroline of the School Sisters of Notre Dame. The Sisters came from Munich to Milwaukee to help keep the German language alive. John Henni was the first German bishop in the U.S. for the newly created Diocese of Milwaukee in 1843. Consecrated bishop on March 19, 1844, Archbishop John Martin Henni worked to bring religious orders into the Milwaukee Diocese, including the Daughters (Sisters) of Charity, the School Sisters of Notre Dame, the School Sisters of St. Francis, the Franciscan Sisters of Penance and Charity, the Jesuits, and the Capuchins. Henni also supported the German and English-language Catholic newspapers.

In Walker's Point, a Catholic Free School was founded in 1850 even before the Holy Trinity Church was completed, because education was so important to the Catholic Germans in the surrounding community.

In 1851, wealthy German-Milwaukee citizens founded the Milwaukee Schulverein (the Milwaukee Educational Association) because they feared the decline of German cultural identity. They established this educational organization to provide quality education in two languages. They built the German-English Academy to provide children with the opportunity to study such innovative areas as singing, drawing, gymnasium, and domestic science classes. Founder Peter Engelmann wanted to create a new school for "our modern times." His personal collection of fossils, minerals,, and plants formed the nucleus of the Milwaukee Public Museum, a natural history museum, the first of its kind in the country.

The German-English Academy joined with the German Teacher's Seminary (Turnlehrer Seminar of the North American Gymnastics Union) in 1876. Due to lack of space, in 1890, and in memory of Guido Pfister, his wife and their daughter, Mrs. Fred Vogel, Jr., donated funds for a new building. During WWI, in 1918, the name was changed to Milwaukee Academy, then to Milwaukee University School (MUS). In 1927, MUS moved from its downtown location to the East Side. Today, after a merger of MUS, Milwaukee Downer Seminary, and Milwaukee Country Day School, the newly named University School of Milwaukee is on a campus in far northeast Milwaukee.

Mathilde F. Anneke began the Milwaukee-Töchter-Institute in 1865. This was a girls-only school, with instruction given exclusively in the German language. The school lasted for 18 years. Anneke was

continued on page 122

Children from some of Milwaukee's most prominent commercial families of the late 1890s attended the private German-English Academy, including Marie Meinicke (toys), Erwin and Herman Uihlein (beer), Ilma Vogel (tannery), and Albert Blatz (beer).

Sei still ......

These well-dressed young men from the German-English Academy/Milwaukee University School in the 1920s include Richard Gust, Frederick Gust, W.F. Mackie, Jr., John Stratton, Albert O. Trostel, Jr., Edward J. Brumder, Charles A. Krause, Jr., Joseph B. Gutenkinst, Harold W. Meyer, James T. Bannen, E. Layton Busby, Paul N. Ruez, Henry F. Furlong, Karl Buehler, Hamilton Riddel, and Albert S. Harvey, Jr.

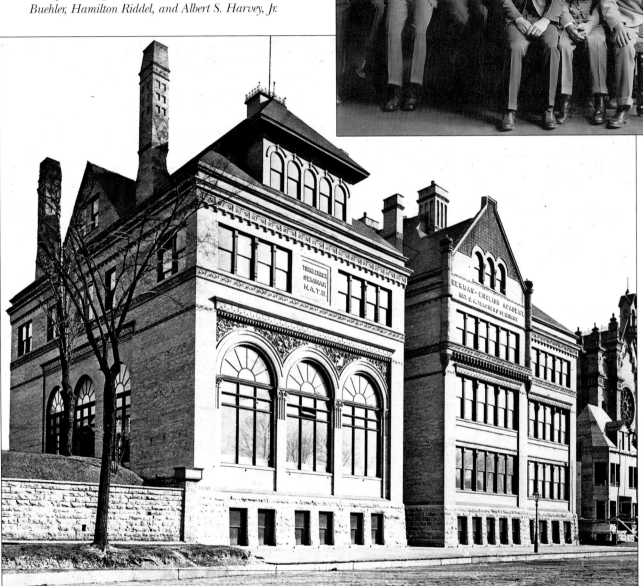

Peter Engelmann, founder of the German-English Academy

This building, constructed in 1890, housed the second German-English Academy.

Be Quiet

121

Milwaukee's first feminist and published *Die Frauen Zeitung* (Women's Times) for a few issues.

In the 1870s, the movement to bring the German-based educational idea of "*Kindergarten*" to America received great support in Milwaukee. Margarethe Schurz opened the first kindergarten in the United States in Watertown, Wisconsin. The idea was so popular that the Milwaukee Public Schools adopted the kindergarten program in 1881.

Prominent wealthy German families (such as the Pritzlaffs, Harnischfegers, Brumders, and Wehrs) of the latter half of the nineteenth century living on the west side of Milwaukee were instrumental in the 1881 founding of Concordia College on West State Street. Now Concordia University, it is located in Mequon, Wisconsin, 15 miles north of downtown Milwaukee.

In 1889, Hans Bruening and Eugene Luening founded The Wisconsin College of Music, now known as The Conservatory, to promote the study of music. Instruction in piano, violin, elocution, oratory, and dramatic arts was offered, as were faculty concerts, student recitals, and chamber music. Today the Conservatory is active in a restored mansion on Prospect Avenue.

Finally, in 1958, socialist mayor Frank P. Zeidler was the first person to receive an honorary doctorate from the University of Wisconsin-Milwaukee.

Louise Schoenleber attended the Second Ward School, shown here in 1904. She and her sister were later directors of the Ambrosia Chocolate Company founded by her father, Otto Schoenleber, in 1894. Ambrosia produces a sizeable share of the bulk chocolate which is used in many sweet products distributed worldwide.

The above picture shows the German-English Academy's graduating class of 1913. The National German-American Teachers' Seminary was comprised of both male and female students.

MILWAUKEE SCHOOL OF ENGINEERING

Oscar Werwath graduated with degrees in both electrical and mechanical engineering in Germany. Following his graduation, Oscar's father financed a trip around the world for his son. When Oscar reached the Milwaukee leg of his trip, he visited a cousin and then promptly called off the rest of his trip, because he saw the industrial potential and at 23 years old, proceeded to make Milwaukee his home. Oscar's work with electric motors created interest among young workers who wanted to learn more about practical electricity. He felt there was a need for a local technical institute and his friends encouraged him to teach. He began informal classes in 1903 with instruction "in the applied science of electrical engineering" for seven students, in what was originally called the "School of Engineering of Milwaukee." The invention of radio sparked the beginning of radio station WSOE in 1925 (now WMSE). A spin-off became WISN, a prominent Milwaukee radio and television station. In 1932, the school's name was changed to "Milwaukee School of Engineering" (MSOE). In 2003, with an enrollment of 2,600 students on a 15-acre campus and 18,000 alumni, MSOE celebrated its 100th anniversary. MSOE has grown phenomenally to become a vital force in providing well-qualified, skilled engineers to Milwaukee's vibrant industrial community. Oscar Werwath's son, Carl, followed him as the school's second President. Robert R. Spitzer was next, and the current President, Herman Vietz, is the fourth German to hold the position.

School of Engineering founder Oscar Werwath drove his own electric-powered vehicle around Milwaukee in 1907. The automotive field was one of his early interests, especially the manufacture of storage batteries for automotive use.

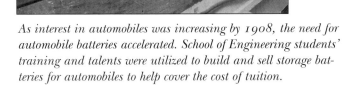

As interest in automobiles was increasing by 1908, the need for automobile batteries accelerated. School of Engineering students' training and talents were utilized to build and sell storage batteries for automobiles to help cover the cost of tuition.

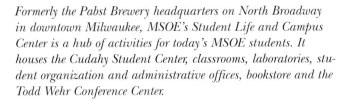

Formerly the Pabst Brewery headquarters on North Broadway in downtown Milwaukee, MSOE's Student Life and Campus Center is a hub of activities for today's MSOE students. It houses the Cudahy Student Center, classrooms, laboratories, student organization and administrative offices, bookstore and the Todd Wehr Conference Center.

GERMAN ORGANIZATIONS

"Much of German social life revolved around churches, musical and athletic societies, free thinking organizations, horticultural societies, cultural clubs, the socialist press, and the informal institutions of the beer hall and neighborhood tavern. All helped assimilate Germans within their own communities and in making the transition from European to American society easier and more pleasant."

A member of the Schlaraffia Society stands proudly in his regalia. Originally founded in 1859, by artists and academics in Prague, the goal was to create an escape for men from the worries of life. Above all, its main purpose was to foster art, humor, and friendship. Exclusively for men of a more mature age and in secure positions, this was not a club for the everyday worker. Members satirized everyday life and recited literary and musical works in witty German prose and verse.

The first Freie Gemeinde *(Free Thinkers) organization built a center in 1870 on 4th Street in Milwaukee (below). In 1928, it moved to the Jefferson Hall on Fond du Lac Avenue, also in Milwaukee (left). Free Thinkers opposed religious creeds, while upholding doctrines of rationalism, science, and humanism. The Jefferson Hall was the hub of most German activity, although not exclusive to the Free Thinkers. It had upper and lower halls for dances, parties, and performances; rehearsal rooms for the singing societies; German language instruction; and a two-lane bowling alley in the lower level. At this venue the German experience endured and flourished.*

Greetings from Milwaukee.
Gruss aus Milwaukee.

FREETHINKER'S HALL   FREIE GEMEINDE-HALLE

While in many cases women were considered the backbone of the family, many were also involved in organizations outside of the home. Alumni groups, ladies auxiliary clubs, and book clubs were places where women shared their thoughts and ideas.

Gentlemen met after long work hours to socialize as well as to discuss business, philanthropic plans, to guide benevolent organizations and to "network." Not having today's technology available, face-to-face meetings were essential.

During this era, picnics were a favored way to spend leisure time with friends and family. Games, food, and of course, beer were each a part of these mini-celebrations.

Members of the Press Club pose for a photo at the Villa Brumder in Pine Lake, Wisconsin. Half of Milwaukee's ten daily papers were published in German. They included the Volksfreund, Abendpost, Seebote, Herold, Germania, Leader, *and* Vorwärts *to name a few.*

THE ERA FROM WORLD WAR I TO THE 1950S

While the early stages of WWI raged in Europe, those Milwaukeeans who still had family in Germany naturally sympathized with their relatives' plight. These sympathies elicited compassion and a desire to help not only a war-torn nation, but their family members specifically. While these Milwaukeeans – many first-generation immigrants themselves – were not wealthy, they longed to help brothers and sisters, mothers and fathers, cousins, aunts and uncles who lived in a worse situation in a war-ravaged country. These Milwaukee families sent packages of food, clothing and shoes, along with cigarettes, and cigars.

Meanwhile, anti-German sentiment swept the United States. In Milwaukee and all over, Germans were the "Hun;" Germans were "the enemy;" Germans were increasingly "bad." In 1917, when the United States entered the war, this unpopularity grew to a head and abruptly, everything German ceased to be recognizable. In Milwaukee, German signs were taken down, and the spoken language changed from German to English. Suddenly, it was not acceptable to be openly or publicly German. As a result, the Deutscher Club became the Wisconsin Club. Beethoven and Wagner were eliminated from all symphonic (and other) concert programs. The Pabst Theater not only canceled its German plays, it suspended one entire season. Lucius Nieman, editor of the *Milwaukee Journal*, probed the local German press and German organizations and subsequently won a 1919 Pulitzer Prize for meritorious service in reporting the sentiment and attitude of Milwaukee Germans regarding the world situation. Between 1919-1923, Pabst Park, which had been Schützen Park, became Garfield Park (and it is now Rose Park!). Attitudes changed and most Americans hid their German background because of the strong negative feelings. Thus, the war accelerated the decline of the city's pro-German reputation.

Fast forward two decades and the situation repeats itself: on the brink of entering WWII, anti-German sentiment entangled itself with anti-Nazi feelings. Once again, all things "German" were "bad." However, while the appearance of "German-ness" was "bad," businesses owned by Americans-of-German-ancestry significantly contributed to United States' war effort. For example, Milwaukee tanneries made shoe leather for soldiers; Milwaukee-based Phoenix Hosiery Company manufactured silk parachutes; Milwaukee's Falk Company made gears for Navy ships; and Milwaukee shipyards contributed to the war effort.

Returning to the post-WWI era, the 18th Amendment enacting Prohibition threw a wrench into many of Milwaukee's manufacturing businesses. The beer industry was the obvious "loser" during Prohibition, but all of the supporting businesses endured hardship – farmers who grew grains had no where to sell them; mills who processed the grains had no outlets; glassmakers had no market for their bottles; and paper board manufacturers could not sell their cartons to the breweries. Consequently, the amendment threw the Milwaukee labor market into chaos. While no breweries were permitted to produce beer, some managed to switch production to soda, while others made flavored soda, cheese, candy bars, and even snow plows, thereby preserving some employees' jobs. However, many breweries were forced to close.

During the 1920s, the federal government severely limited the number of immigrants who could gain entry into the United States. As such, fewer Germans were allowed to come to America than ever before. Many were so desperate to leave the terrible post-WWI conditions in Germany that virtually anywhere else was deemed better. America was – and had been believed to be – the "Land of Opportunity." Yet, those immigrants who were allowed to enter the U.S. found that the streets were not "paved with gold." While the 1920s was a great time for the affluent, working class Americans still needed to work – if they could find jobs.

In 1929, the Stock Market crashed, sending not only the United States, but also most of the world into a massive Depression. The 1930s were bleak for many Americans, and for those of German ancestry, increasingly tense. The scene in Europe radically changed with the rise of Nazism in Germany. As international sentiment became polarized, citizens were called upon to examine their loyalties.

At the time, most Americans of German descent were acquiring U.S. citizenship and regarding themselves as Americans first: American-Germans. Some people, however, kept their primary loyalties with Germany, and considered themselves to be German-American-Germans. These people either left the United States of their own volition and returned to Germany or were escorted out of this country by the American Government.

In 1935, German industry recruited skilled Milwaukee craftsmen of German descent to move to Germany with offers of jobs in Third Reich factories. About 200 families gave up their homes in Milwaukee for jobs in the industrial cities of Germany. Nationwide, 9,000 experienced workers relocated their families from the United States to Germany.

Milwaukeean Mildred Fish married German Arvid Harnack and moved to Germany in 1930. While there, the couple led internal opposition to Hitler while Arvid worked for the Third Reich Economics Ministry. Arrested in 1942, Mildred was the only American-born person known to have been executed by the Gestapo by direct order of Hitler in 1943.

Throughout the war, there was an uncertain feeling in the air – suspicion about a German background was pervasive, and all "Germans" in Milwaukee lived under a cloud. Were they spies? Did they support Hitler? Were the packages sent to Germany containing money to fund the Nazis? Not likely, but in wartime, everything is suspect.

An intriguing and fascinating yet little known aspect of WWII is the internment of Americans of German ancestry. Between 1942-1945, thousands of German aliens and German-Americans were arrested, interned, excluded, paroled, exchanged, and generally harassed by a suspicious country.

"I remember when the FBI or a similar governmental representative knocked on our door when we lived on Upper Third Street in the 1930s and the 1940s. They interrogated both my father and mother, separately, about their allegiance to the United States. Then they went next door to my mother's sister and her husband; then to my mother's brother and his wife; then to our friends and others.

It seemed everyone we knew was visited. We knew one young man who was deported."

Toward the end of WWII several thousand German prisoners of war were brought to Camp Billy Mitchell Field in Milwaukee. As prisoners, they were better off here: they weren't being shot at and they were given good food. They worked – for pay – making small batteries and as laborers on surrounding farms.

The war brought shortages, rations and hardships, but despite all of this, there was also a spirit of upholding German heritage and traditions. The German language school continued to teach German, and Germans gathered for dances, concerts and theatrical performances. Milwaukee Germans, as a group, were not embarrassed to be German; they did not consider themselves to be second-class citizens, but they certainly did not flaunt their "German-ness."

Following the war, the returning servicemen reinvigorated the local economy. Once again, care packages were sent from Milwaukee Germans to family members in post-war Germany. During the early 1950s the next wave of German immigrants arrived. Over the years they found work and many have been very successful in their endeavors.

Three girls are dressed in traditional tracht.

GROWING UP GERMAN

If someone grew up German in Milwaukee, he or she would have a difficult time remembering when his or her parents attended a social gathering without them. Indeed, social life in German Milwaukee was a family affair. German parents expected their children to behave, and those children did, no matter the setting. As such, there was rarely a need for a babysitter (what was that?) and then, only a relative was entrusted with the care of the little ones. Otherwise, children went along with the family to a friend's house where the men usually played *Schafskopf* (sheepshead), the women gossiped and prepared the absolute highlight of the evening: midnight lunch. "Midnight lunch" usually consisted of *Kalter Aufschnitt* (cold cuts), *Hackfleisch* (beef tartare), *Sauere Gurken* (pickles), *Roggenbrodt* (dark rye bread), *Kartoffelsalat* (potato salad), and *Apfel* or *Heidelbeer Kuchen* (apple

This girl, holding a rosary, scrolled certificate, and flower, poses in her family's regional special occasion dress.

Der Weihnachtsbaum *(Christmas Tree)*, with presents scattered around, crossed the ocean to become a symbol of the holidays–even today.

Two typical Milwaukee girls smile for the camera in 1936.

This little girl stops to "smell the roses" on her way to the Schwaben Picnic at Old Heidelberg Park in 1962.

Auf glücklichen zeiten!

or blueberry tart). Children played until they were so tired that they snuggled in blankets or coats and slept wherever until it was time to walk (or be carried) home.

Mealtime, usually by the clock, was a family ritual not to be taken lightly. Punctually seated at the table, with neatly combed hair and freshly washed hands and faces, these respectful children were seen and not heard. Conversation, if any, happened after the meal was eaten. These discussions were frequently endless, and often served as a stimulating delay tactic to postpone washing the dishes.

When there was company, children were especially polite, speaking only when spoken to. Children only addressed adults with *Herr* (Mr.) or *Frau* (Mrs.) or, if familiar, with *Onkel* (uncle) or *Tante* (aunt). Indeed, children never addressed any elder by their first names, and further, never interrupted anyone speaking. Rather, they always stood when an adult entered the room and remained standing until adults were seated. Then, there was the obligatory handshake, which accompanied

every greeting and every farewell.

Deutsche Musik (German music) filled the airwaves. One special radio hour reigned at 6 p.m. every evening. "It was our dance lesson time. When Papa felt we'd learned the steps for the waltz or polka or two-step (and/or he'd had enough dancing), he gave us the broom in his place, a book on the head for balancing, and we practiced as long as the music played. We were going to be ready to dance at the next dance party."

Saturday mornings were reserved for *Deutsche Schule,* (German School) where Frau Dora Grunewald taught an appreciation of knowing another language, pronunciation, understanding poems, singing songs "with feeling" and *lauter* (louder). We practiced and practiced for the next *Weihnachts Programm* (Christmas Program) where many parents, with tear-filled eyes, applauded their children who so sweetly sang the Christmas favorites – among them, *O, Tannenbaum, Ihr Kinderlein Kommet,* and *Stille Nacht.*

The First Holy Communion Candle is a memorable keepsake for young Catholics.

Prom is timeless —anticipated, enjoyed and remembered.

These cousins take a break from their playing to pose at the Schwaben Picnic at Old Heidelberg Park in 1962.

"Fritzi," the German Fest mascot, is pictured hugging a small girl wearing a dirndl in 1999.

To happy times!

MUSIC AND THE ARTS

During the late 1800s, Milwaukee was a city of music, filled with a strong German-American community that supported numerous musical societies and groups. As early as 1850, a Musikverein von Milwaukee (Milwaukee Musical Society) was formed. In 1858, the choral Milwaukee Liedertafel was founded, followed by the Milwaukee Liederkranz in 1878, and the Schwaben Männerchor in the 1880s. These male choruses sang a wide repertoire of songs from German *Lieder* to German drinking songs. They gave public concerts every year, even during the first and second world wars. They performed with other German choruses at periodic statewide *Sängerfests*, or songfests,

the first of which was in 1862; as well as at national *Sängerfests*; and even at today's German Fest Milwaukee. While there were many other *Männerchöre* (Men's Choruses) in Milwaukee throughout the years, these remain active today.

In 1851, merely three years after Wisconsin's statehood, traveling and local companies performed German plays in Milwaukee. From 1865 onward, there were stock company productions, minstrel shows, dramatic performances and gorgeous spectacles at the Music Hall. These performances helped establish a foundational basis for today's varied theatrical groups in Milwaukee. In 1868, Jacob Nunnemacher

built Milwaukee's first Opera House, a lavish and ornate 1,000 seat venue. It opened in 1871 with the opera *Martha*. Captain Fredrick Pabst bought the opera house in 1890 and renamed it Stadt Theater. Afterwards, the German Repertory Theater Company performed plays there. After the fire in 1893, it was rebuilt on its same site on Wells Street, once again incorporating elaborate interior decorations with super acoustics. In addition, it has no columns or supports to obstruct the view of the stage. When the English productions didn't draw audiences, a German theater group took over and enjoyed immense popularity from 1893 through the First World War.

This poster advertises the Erstes Diletanten Blaeser Quartett des Musikvereins *(the First Amateur Brass Quartet of the Music Society).*

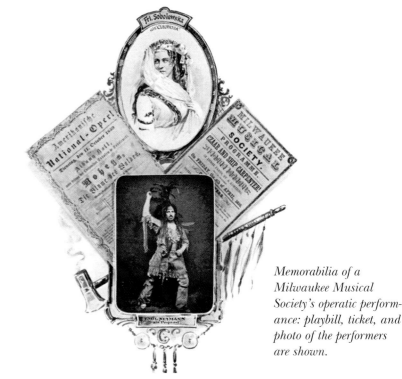

Memorabilia of a Milwaukee Musical Society's operatic performance: playbill, ticket, and photo of the performers are shown.

*A larger band, the Pabst Drum Corps, is a brewery-sponsored group of musicians
who played at brewery events and other functions. Note their stylish uniforms!*

Christoph (Christian) Bach began his famous orchestra in 1855. It was the only symphony orchestra in Milwaukee for more than half a century, and was famous throughout the Midwest. The year 1865 saw a leading-edge Academy of Music established in Milwaukee, and in 1899, the Wisconsin College of Music was established. The latter's Mozart Hall was the site of many recitals and receptions. It later became the Conservatory of Music to serve the interests of music students. In 1890, Franz Mayr established a Military band and Orchestra which offered free public band concerts in city parks and was a popular source of entertainment through 1920. Further, 1906 saw the advent of a German brass band, *Musik Kapelle Einigkeit Verein*, which was in great demand for parties, picnics, festivals, dance halls, and beer parlors. These companies are just a few of many various musical groups.

In 1906, Milwaukee celebrated half a century of Christoph (Christian) Bach's talents. In his address, Milwaukee Mayor David S. Rose stated "...no man has ever done more for the city of Milwaukee than Mr. Bach and his orchestra."

This 1904 photograph of the Milwaukee Bandonian Trio represents yet another facet of the German Milwaukee musical scene. Trios, quartets, sextets, small bands, and orchestras performed throughout the Milwaukee area in addition to the larger symphonies, orchestras, and bands of the era.

Alte Ansiedler der Westseite *(the Westside Old Settler's Band) is yet another example of a local community band shown here at Blatz Park in 1914.*

In 1922, the Beihoff Novelty Orchestra broadcast over WIAO, a newly formed radio station. Norbert Beihoff was founder and chairman of Beihoff Music Corp, which is still expanding in Milwaukee today. In 1925, WIAO was taken over by Milwaukee School of Engineering's WSOE. The station and the school gained recognition when national figures took part in the programs, including Col. Charles Lindbergh and President Hoover. Some other musical organizations in Milwaukee included a *Deutsches Männerquartett*, a Philharmonic Society, and a Concertina Club, begun by Fred and Adolph Buettner. Today, Art Altenburg's Concertina Bar, on Milwaukee's South Side, continues the tradition of featuring everything concertina: music, singing, and dancing. Also, over 74 concertinas are on display.

Turnverein Milwaukee Drum Corps performed at many events including Fasching *(German Mardi Gras), parties, weddings, dances, receptions, and parades.*

The United German Male Singing Choruses of Milwaukee held a benefit concert to aid the suffering in Germany and Austria on March 7, 1920, in the Milwaukee Auditorium.

One of many Männerchöre, *men's choruses, such as this proudly sing a wide variety of musical selections. They are still enjoying the* Gemütlichkeit *their singing brings to each other as well as to others. Over 127 years of demonstrating their pride in their German heritage has not diminished their zeal. There was* Männerchöre *for men,* Damenchöre *for women, and* Kinderchöre *for children. German song for everyone.* √

The Wisconsin Symphony Orchestra exemplified the best of the best, performing here at the Pabst Theater. Today, concerts of the Milwaukee Symphony Orchestra are given in Uihlein Hall of the Marcus Center for the Performing Arts in downtown Milwaukee.

Some members of the Milwaukee Zither Club perform at the Jefferson Hall.

What a delightful afternoon at the park it must have been — to sing along with the folksongs and familiar tunes of the Milwaukee Zither Club.

Wilhelm Bintner plays the zither at his Golden Zither Restaurant. Billed at the time as "America's most authentic German restaurant," former patrons recall enjoying Alpine melodies, which brought back memories of their homeland.

The phonograph was a desirable and treasured item used to listen to German records and American recordings of German songs, both instrumental and vocal. When it needed attention, a skilled repairman was available for service.

Many of the aforementioned band and orchestra members played handcrafted instruments. Here, a Milwaukee artisan crafts a violin.

GERMAN PAINTERS

The rich cultural heritage of the German immigrants fostered a great respect for the work of artists. These included painters, sculptors, glass and metal crafters, woodcarvers, authors, needle-workers and, of course, musicians. Examples of their work are abundant throughout the city. Today local museums house much of the best of their work.

The Milwaukee Art Museum (MAM) holds a strong German Impressionists col-lection, in addition to the Von Schleinitz Collection of German paintings and ceramics. In 1991, Richard and Erna Flagg donated their incredible collection of German art to MAM. Another generous supporter of the arts, Eckhard Grohman, owns an extensive art collection entitled "Man at Work" which is now housed at the Milwaukee School of Engineering.

Among the many authors who supplied publishers with endless material was poet Konrad Krez, a '48er and lawyer, who became Milwaukee's City Attorney. He wrote inspiring poems about his homeland and new home.

The most elaborate and impressive art project in Milwaukee in the late 19th century was the Panorama paintings whose painters came mostly from Germany. Although the popularity of the Panoramic paintings lasted only 20 years, Milwaukee was known as the Panorama Center of the World during that era.

The Panoramic painters worked collaboratively on works so large that they used 18,000 square feet of linen. A canvas could be 50-foot high and 400-foot around. Each painter had his specialty. One did trees and distances, the other skies. Another painted animals, another people, while yet another worked on horses. The price for such a grand piece of work was $25,000.

The Battle of Atlanta, *painted in Milwaukee, is the only known Panorama painting still in existence today and is located in a specially constructed Cyclorama building (built in 1921) in Atlanta, Georgia.*

Henry Vianden, painter and teacher, who taught von Marr, was famous for his historical scenes. These painters helped spawn one of Milwaukee's nicknames, "little Munich."

Carl von Marr is considered by many to be one of the best German artists. Born in Milwaukee, he studied and painted in Germany. His immense 13-foot by 25-foot canvas of his masterpiece, The Flagellants, *was completed in 1889, and won a prize at the 1893 Chicago Worlds Fair. It and other von Maur paintings can be seen currently at the West Bend Art Museum.*

At William Wehner's Panorama Shop, scaffolding was erected for the painters to access the upper portions of the panoramas. When the Panorama paintings were viewed, a platform was built for viewing.

Richard Lorenz was a Panorama painter who contributed to the art scene in Milwaukee. The artists worked on such large paintings that they did not use brushes, but instead applied the paint using knives.

Robert Schade, Richard Lorenz, Otto von Ernst, Emily Groom, Charlotte Partridge, Alexander Mueller, George Raab, Elsa Ulbricht and Robert von Neumann are all prominent Wisconsin artists, some of whom made it possible for the next generation of artists born here to receive adequate training. Among the latter are Fred Berman, Joseph Friebert, Ruth Grotenrath, Carl Holz, Schomer Lichtner, Mathilde Schley, Robert Shellin, and Edward Steichen as well as Paul Hammersmith (etchings) and Alfred Sessler (block prints).

This keepsake is from the Künstler Heim *(the Artists' Home) in Milwaukee. Some artists lived there, and others visited. They were warmly welcomed and entertained each other with discussions about their work and debated the issues of the day.*

Erinnerung an die Altdeutsche Trinkstube

Memories of the Old German Drinking Room

Frank Enders, shown in his Milwaukee studio, was the only native Milwaukeean among the Panorama painters. He was very prolific artist.

This house is an example of Fachwerkbau *(half-timber framed). It was built by Robert Machek, an Austrian woodcarver, carpenter and cabinetmaker between the years of 1873-1894. A striking example of "old world" craftsmanship, it remains an unusual residence on North Nineteenth Street in Milwaukee. Some believe the iron fence around the property was made by Cyril Colnik. The artist of the image is unknown.*

Schomer Lichtner, the dean of Wisconsin artists, is best known for his expressive and whimsical paintings of ballerinas and dairy cows. As a young man, Lichtner painted for the WPA during the Roosevelt Administration. He created murals depicting American Indians and pioneers local to Wisconsin. He had a long and artistically productive life.

Cyril Colnik, born in 1871 in Austria, is known as Milwaukee's best ironwork craftsman. At the World Columbian Exposition of 1893 in Chicago, his masterwork of a gargoyle (shown here) won the best of show prize. He settled in Milwaukee and his metal working shop eventually employed up to 25 people. Villa Terrace houses his collection, but fine examples of his work may be seen on fences and gates throughout the city.

LEISURE TIME

A distinctive attribute of the German-American was a rich and well-organized social life. As early as 1840, local and visiting theatrical groups performed plays. Concerts, musical instrument clubs (mandolin, violin, etc.), opera, and male choruses (such as the *Liedertafel*) enriched the cultural life of the city by providing music in its many forms. Artists, such as the Panorama painters, the wrought iron and glass artisans, and the landscape and park system developers all contributed to the rich quality of life which everyone enjoyed.

Athletic organizations, such as gymnastics, fencing, soccer, and sharpshooting clubs; chess and checkers clubs; *Skat* (an intricate card game) and *Schafskopf* (Sheepshead) were popular in leisure time. Further, one in five Germans belonged to a *Turnverein* (Turners Gymnastics Organization).

Added to these leisure activities, of course, were the beer gardens and taverns. From Reuthlisberger's first brewery (established in 1841) to three dozen breweries built through 1900 to the micro breweries of today, beer and its related businesses have been major components in the fabric of Milwaukee. Taverns, beer halls, bars – no matter what you call them – were places where immigrants could go. There they could sit and talk, absorb their new community, and digest the good and the bad. Above all, the drinking establishments were places that fostered community among strangers.

An interesting highlight of the early 20th century was the *Deutsches Kino* (German movie house). It showed German language films and reminded the audience of home. Additionally, it kept the German language alive for subsequent generations. Conversely, to improve their limited English, German immigrants went to the English language movies to hear the spoken language and learn idioms, expressions, and speech patterns.

The Ebner Brothers pose here for a family photo at the billiards table, a favorite pastime in a cozy tavern.

The annual *Jahrmarkt* (the Yearly Market) was akin to a county fair. The street fair featured exhibits, produce, handicrafts, food, and amusements including a carousel, amusement rides, a "flying carnival ride," bowling, billiards, and cigars. In the spring, the counterpart to the *Jahrmarkt* was the *Mai Fest* (May Festival), a traditional celebration greeting the arrival of spring to which the Germans invited "their fellow citizens at large." Germans love to celebrate, and for eight years, beginning in 1933, the lakefront hosted a grand midsummer festival. It was an annual pageant with spectacular fireworks and free local talent. People participating in this festival prior to WWII remembered it fondly in later years, and some believe this mid-summer festival was an early version of the later (and current) Summerfest.

This Jahrmarkt *was held on National Avenue in late summer. The entryway (photo above) is reminiscent of an old-world gate tower, inviting visitors with a big* Willkommen *(welcome).*

Männerchöre *(Mens Choruses) hosted* Sängerfeste *(Singer Fests) wherein each group competed against the others, but mostly participated for the camaraderie at this lavishly presented event. At the end, following the competition, as was customary, they joined together to give a very spirited performance for their audience.*

143

There were Fourth of July parades everywhere. Milwaukee's celebrations of the Fourth included this popular Doll and Buggy group, anxiously waiting to begin (right). In the photo above a *1885* horse-drawn float, including costumed participants (both human and equine), was seen at Old National Avenue Park, west of 27th Street. Werner's Hats sponsored a decorated car in a later parade (top right). The young ladies in the car are wearing the latest fashionable hats.

A "hot" 62 degrees Fahrenheit was the highest maximum temperature for January 26, 1944, the warmest ever recorded in Milwaukee. The Mueller family took advantage of the balmy weather and enjoyed a picnic at Carl Schurz Park in Grafton!

Prosit! *A German toast to having a good time.*

The Berlin Arcade Building housed amusements and Rice's Hall, wherein the Milwaukee Concertina Circle rehearsed in 1889. This orchestra included cornets, trombones, violins, a xylophone, and other instruments as well as concertinas. They played at parks, beer gardens, and dances throughout Milwaukee. Rosenberg's Clothing Store later occupied this space.

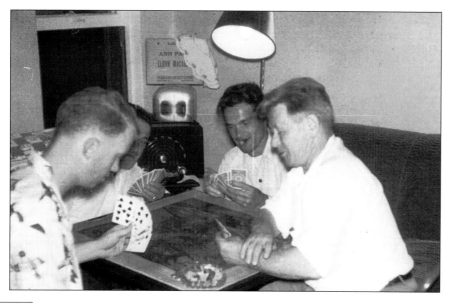

Herbie, 13, and sister Caroline Schiller, 11, are young members of the Holzhacker Buam *(Woodchopper Boys), a Bavarian dance group. They are shown here in 1945 at the Holiday Folk Fair.*

Willie Knauss and friends often played Schafskopf *(Sheepshead) in the 1950s. Privately, friends got together and played* Skat, Euchre, *poker, or other card games. While the men played cards in the basement, their wives spent the time in the kitchen, preparing "lunch" – no matter the time of day. Publically, groups hosted benefit card parties in clubs, halls, and hotels. Ladies embroidered and crocheted pillowcases and other items for prizes.*

OCT. 24, 1937

768-B

MAYER STUDIO 2

The entire Deutschen Schützen Club posed onstage at the Jefferson Hall before their theatre group performed a play, "'S Annerl vom Grundhof."

Schneewittchen und die sieben Zwerge (*Snow White and the Seven Dwarves*), *a three-act play, was produced by a theatrical group using children who were pupils at the Saturday German School. The afternoon performance was held at the Jefferson Hall in 1943; food and dance followed.*

Miller Theater on 3rd Street, North of Grand Avenue (Wisconsin Avenue), went from staging vaudeville variety acts to theatrical plays.

German plays were presented at the Schubert Theater (Academy of Music) as early as 1851. Opera and theatre stars from Germany performed here. It was considered to be the leading German language stage west of New York.

Milwaukee has a rich tradition of theater. The first local theatrical group began in 1850. Traveling theatrical troupes have performed in the city since 1851. *Der Deutscher Theater Verein* (The German Theater Club) produced many delightful plays and operettas (left). The cast (below left) of *Der Schützen Verein* (the Sharpshooters Club) posed here for a photograph following one of their many performances. And these two ladies (below) are all dressed up for a *Fasching* (Mardi Gras) party. In addition to the annual *Fasching*, "Hard Times" parties were popular in the 1930s. People dressed like hobos to distract themselves from the realities of everyday life. Later, masquerades became fashionable.

Woody Herman, born in Milwaukee of German parents, was a jazz singer, an accomplished instrumentalist, and leader of one of the Big Band orchestras.

The nightclub chanteuse "The Incomparable Hildegarde" was perhaps the quintessential American dinner and supper club entertainer. A German-American, she grew up in Milwaukee and was a classically trained pianist. Her personal "signature look" included long white gloves. Hildegarde retired in 1998 at the age of 89, after performing for decades and constantly reinventing herself and her musical style. In the '40s, she was on radio; in the '50s and '60s she was "one of the most popular cabaret acts in the world," and in the '70s she was on Broadway in the cast of Follies. In 1986, she celebrated 60 years in show business in front of a sell-out crowd at Carnegie Hall. She was on the cover of Life magazine and Revlon introduced a Hildegarde shade of lipstick and nail polish. She died at age 99, after becoming a Third Order Carmelite nun.

During the 1930s and 1940s, Heinie and his Grenadiers was a band which featured performances of German folk music on its regular radio broadcasts. At noon each day, the sirens would sound, signifying the 12 pm lunch hour for many workers in the city of Milwaukee. Many of these day laborers looked forward to the lunch whistle, because it proclaimed the beginning of the Heinie Radio Hour on WTMJ.

TAVERNS

"....where everybody knows your name ...."

The Milwaukee House Tavern was also a boardinghouse. Men always entered the front door of taverns, while some taverns had family entrances on the side for wives and families who were not allowed to enter through the front door.

In Germany, every small village or town had a *Gasthaus* or *Wirtschaft* (restaurant or tavern) where many of the people went to socialize. They brought this "institution" with them, and it is said that, "Milwaukee has a bar and church on almost every corner." People did not necessarily go to the bars and taverns for the alcohol; they went to visit and socialize. Early on, only men were allowed in the bars; later, entire families went to the tavern for entertainment, to sing and enjoy the music, chat with others and for *Gemütlichkeit* (conviviality).

♪ *Ein Prosit, ein Prosit,*
der Gemütlichkeit.
Ein Prosit, ein Prosit,
der Gemütlichkeit.
Eins, Zwei, Drei, G'SUFFA!

Cheer! Cheer!
to a good time.
Cheers! Cheers!
to a good time.
One, Two, Three, DRINK! ♪

These celebrating men are part of the '39ers Club of the Milwaukee Turners.

This is a typical "stand-up" bar for working men, where the saloonkeepers offered free food to entice customers.

Regular patrons visited their favorite taverns even on Christmas (here in *1908*). It was customary for the owner to treat the guests on the holiday.

This saloon features a very large advertisement on its side, as did many.

"Im Himmel, gibt's kein Bier"

In heaven, there ain't no beer;
That's why we drink it here;
And when we're gone from here,
Our friends will be drinking all the beer!

Corners seemed to have attracted taverns, probably because the owners like the exposure, unlike residences, which tend to prefer privacy. The Blue Ribbon Buffet in Wauwatosa (below left) is a great architectural example of the "corner" tavern. While the Peter Holtz Beer Hall, circa 1885, (below right) is another.

The Blue Ribbon Buffet in Wauwatosa was a friendly place for many in the neighborhood.

Peter Holtz Beer Hall, circa 1885, located next to the Davidson Theater.

Herman Toser and John Schickel each enjoy a glass of imported wine at their wholesale import wine business in their Weinkeller (wine cellar), which they operated from 1880-1920. With Prohibition, the business changed to provide spirits to city drug stores, hospitals, and first aid stations (for medicinal purposes, of course). From 1860-1890 Heinrich Lieber's winery produced wine from locally grown grapes, currants, and elderberries.

Jetzt trinken wir noch ein Glas Wein
(Now, let's drink another glass of wine)

…tablecloths in "modern" times; spittoons on the floor of yesteryear's taverns…

 "Trink, Trink, Brüderlein, Trink!"

Trink! Trink, Brüderlein, trink!
Lass doch die Sorgen zu Haus.
Meide den Kummer und meide den Schmerz,
Dann ist das Leben ein Scherz!
Meide den Kummer und meide den Schmerz,
Dann ist das Leben ein Scherz!

Drink! Drink, brother, drink!
Leave your sorrows at home.
Forget your worries and forget your pain,
Then life is a joke!
Forget your worries and forget your pain,
Then life is a joke!

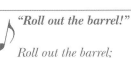 *"Roll out the barrel!"*

Roll out the barrel;
We've got the blues on the run.
Zing, Boom, Terrarral;
Sing out a song of good cheer..
Now's the time to roll out the barrel,
For the gang's all here!

BEER HALLS

Milwaukee's drinking establishments varied in size from the neighborhood taverns, to the somewhat larger beerhalls, to the largest, the Jefferson Hall. The beerhalls served as gathering places for wedding receptions, *Sangverein* (Chorus) parties, *Kirchweihfest* (after-church harvest festival), concerts, and family get-togethers. Taverns, beer gardens, and beer halls all served as a meeting place to have a meal, play cards, or play organized sports. These were places where strangers were turned into friends. Families as well as single individuals all spent time – together – in the beer halls.

Germans love the outdoors and enjoy gardens, whether in their own backyards, or in private or public parks. The beautifully designed Milwaukee Gardens also incorporated a beer hall, another German favorite.

The Forst Keller, a former Methodist Church, was a popular venue for socializing near the Pabst Brewery.

A SPOT that will linger in the memory of Milwaukeeans and guests of Milwaukee for many years. This is the Schlitz hotel palm garden, formerly located on the southeast corner of Third-st and Grand-av, and the center of night life in days gone by.

A. I. Cross photo.

The exterior of the Schlitz Hotel Palm Garden is impressive (above), as was the interior (left photo). Established in 1896, it was famous for its year-round garden, concerts, parties, dances, and other entertainment. The lavish interior included potted plants, statuary, art work, and electric illumination of the arches. Seating capacity was 900, with live musicians in red coats playing background and dancing music. A coin-operated Wurtlitzer Orchestron played melodies after hours. As a companion to the Palm Garden, Schlitz also built the Tivoli Palm Garden on South 5th Street in 1901. In it were a bar, café, dance hall, bowling alley, and barbershop.

SETTING THE TABLE

German-American farmers grew grains, fruits, and vegetables and kept chickens, pigs, horses, and cattle. Many also grew cash crops such as wheat for flour and hops for beer to sell in urban markets. They needed mills to grind their wheat, banks to lend them money, schools to teach their children, stores to sell them dry goods, blacksmiths to make their tools, and churches and/or taverns to soothe their souls. Any place where these necessities of life could be gathered at a water source or railroad crossing, a rural village sprang to life. Some became cities, such as Milwaukee.

But what did the early farmers grow? What did the early immigrants eat? It certainly took a few years to accumulate cash to purchase livestock. In the interim, many German immigrants subsisted on garden produce, wild game, fish, berries, apples, and the wild rice that grew in some marshy areas—essentially, whatever was available.

Rye was a popular grain in Germany; however, the soil of southeastern Wisconsin made wheat an easier crop to grow. On the one hand, this was good for the farmers, because in the old country white bread (wheat bread) could only be bought by wealthier families and it meant that here they were "wealthy." On the other hand, some liked rye bread and missed it.

The Jahrmarkt *was held annually at the end of summer, early fall. Aside from wonderful fresh produce, the vendors sold other handicrafts. Amusements and games were located on the grounds as well. Children would delight at the flying carnival ride, while the men could appreciate the billiards and cigars.*

Der Grünermarkt *(the green market) was "The clearing house for table food and conversation." A daily event, farmers would come and sell their seasonal produce. Fruits, vegetables, eggs,* Schmierkäse *(spread cheese), and* Spanferkel *(roast pig) were all popular foods for sale at the market.*

Commission Row was where grocers purchased their produce early each day to be sold later in their shops, when customers shopped for their daily food. People needed to shop daily because there was no refrigeration in the home.

Families typically lived upstairs and worked downstairs in the family store. The Trondles posed outside in their standard, long, fresh white aprons.

STEINMEYER

William Steinmeyer, Captain of the 26th Wisconsin Infantry, became a grocer.

William Steinmeyer, born in Germany, came to Milwaukee with his parents at age six. A gunsmith by trade, he enlisted in the 26th Wisconsin Infantry and fought in the Civil War. Upon his return, he opened a retail grocery with a partner, and based on a cash-only philosophy, took orders on one day and delivered on the next. Steinmeyer bought out his partner in 1877, thereby becoming the sole proprietor. Soon after, he built his own new, brick grocery store. He died in 1892, and his son-in-law, Emil H. Ott, took over with his step-brother, Charles. They continued the business until 1946, when the Milwaukee institution known as Steinmeyer's closed. The former Steinmeyer's Grocery site is today located on Old World Third Street and Highland Avenue.

Steinmeyer's is remembered for its vast array of specialty foods. In addition to the regular staples, it featured fresh fish, unusual condiments, fancy candies, assorted wines, and special blends of coffees–even blended to taste. The most unusual feature at Steinmeyer's was when you paid for an item or an order, the money traveled in a little wire cage to the cashier on the second floor. Change and receipts were returned in the same manner.

Steinmeyer began his grocery business by making personal deliveries with a wheelbarrow or carrying sacks of groceries on his back. He eventually grew out of this first building into something bigger.

Customers would place cash orders in return for a promise of next day delivery "Please, don't ask for credit … we sell for cash only."

Upper right: Later, Steinmeyer added a lunch counter to better serve his customers.

Steinmeyer's large fleet of delivery trucks clearly indicates the magnitude of the grocer's business.

NOV. 24, 1924.

This photo represents the interior of virtually any grocer of the time– pyramid stacked cans; clerks standing at attention awaiting customers; a large pickle jar; burlap bags of sugar and flour; and coffee beans waiting to be freshly ground.

Retzer Brothers Quality Grocers, located at 6th and Mineral, delivered groceries and continued the tradition Steinmeyer began.

RETZER BROS. QUALITY GROCERS.

EATING OUT

There is a wide range of cuisine among Germans. During the 19th and 20th centuries, different restaurants prepared dishes according to their owner's regional background, thus making many options available to suit all tastes. Today, there are increasingly fewer German restaurants in Milwaukee, as the populations tastes change to include an ever-widening array of different ethnic foods.

Accustomed to going to the *Gasthaus* (Inn) for community fellowship, German immigrants were naturally drawn to a similar place while living in America. One such American counterpart in Milwaukee was "Mother Heiser's" Restaurant. At the turn of the century, as these German immigrants were acquiring their citizenship, they needed to study to pass the test. "Ma" Heiser's had a backroom stocked with reference books for those studying English and trying to familiarize themselves with American ways.

Hermann's Café, located on Water Street, was a likely spot for the bankers and businessmen who worked in the area to stop, chat, and enjoy a coffee.

While the English had their tea; the Germans had their coffee. Café Martini (1871-1976) was "the" popular meeting place for many locals. Typically, at four in the afternoon, people would stop for coffee and a delicacy from the adjoining bakery. Men enjoyed their coffee at a Stammtisch (a table reserved for regular customers).

163

The Bavarian Wurst Haus, formerly Dietze's Wurst Haus, on West Appleton Avenue in northwest Milwaukee was a favorite restaurant with delicious German fare (top left). Adjoining was a sausage market with imported German specialty items (top right). Chef Norbert Holland followed the fine tradition established by Dietze, whose well-known meat market had been on upper 3rd Street.

John Ernst Café was originally called "Mother Heiser's." Inside this popular German restaurant checkered tablecloths, high wooden beam ceilings, and a huge fireplace created a welcoming atmosphere. Colorful murals also decorated the inside of the John Ernst Café. Below one depicts the owner himself bowing before lavish offerings where the champagne is on ice and the candles are lit.

Kegel's on South 59ᵗʰ Street has murals all around the walls, along with German proverbs and sayings. One of the few remaining restaurant/bars of its kind, Kegel's is popular nowadays for its fish fry and for the welcoming, friendly atmosphere which it has always retained through the years.

National Ave. (Highway 15) at So. 59th Street

See these Colorful German Waitresses at

Glatz's German Kitchen

1107 N. Third Street   Broadway 0499
Milwaukee, Wis.

Glatz's German Kitchen, located on North 3rd Street. Run by John Glatz and his family, Glatz's motto was, "Give 'em good food and plenty to eat."

Schwaben Hof on 12th Street had carved wooden railings, seats, and chairs, and Black Forest charm all around.

Joe Deutsch's Café, located on Galena Street, was another local favorite.

"The Comfort," as Mader's was known in 1902, offered customers free lunch at the bar, often consisting of pickles, pickled onions, and whatever the cook prepared, likely sausage and open-faced sandwiches. Sounds unbelievable, but it was actually a common practice during those times. Today, Mader's is home to the world's largest beer stein, a collection of arms, and beautiful wood-carved murals.

The Bavarian Inn adjoins Old Heidelberg Park and Soccer Fields, in Glendale, a northern Milwaukee suburb. Pictured at the right is the early building. At the left are scenes of the lovely Alpine-style chalet, whose most unique feature is a Kachelofen (tile stove). The scene of many German functions, the Bavarian Inn is the home of five Bavarian societies.

FINE
GERMAN
CUISINE

Bavarian Inn

General Manager Victor Cerda, Chef Joe Deutsch, and staff.

When you first approach the Bavarian Inn, your eyes focus on a 75 foot *Maibaum* (May Pole) outside the front door. The *Maibaum* contains the symbols of and annual events associated with the five local German societies that own this legendary complex. These five original societies are as follows: the Bavarian Soccer Club; the Bayerischer Vergnugungs Club (Bavarian Social Club); the B.G.T.V.D'Lustig'n Wendlstoana, (which fosters the customs and fashions of Old Bavaria); the Gesang Verein Bavaria (Bavarian Singing Society, as founded in 1895); and the S.V.E.V.D'Oberlanders (whose mission is to uphold the traditions of the Bavarian culture and whose name, D'Oberlandler, means the mountain people or highlanders). In 1934, these five societies merged to form the United Bavarian Societies. When they built The Bavarian Inn in 1967, their intention was to create an authentic, detailed replica of a Bavarian Chalet, where they, and the public, could continue the customs and culture of Old Bavaria. Victor Cerda, the Inn's general manager comments, "We at the Bavarian Inn still strive to preserve and celebrate the Bavarian heritage."

In the lobby you can marvel at the *Kachelofen*, a remarkable handcrafted oven built from tile. Passing by glass cases of soccer trophies and Society memorabilia, you enter a dining room filled greatly touched by Bavarian influence. Hand-carved dragon heads support the mantle of the massive stone fireplace. Above that mantle stands the nearly century old sculpture of Konig Gambrinus—the mythical king of beer. Equally ancient carved gargoyles grin at you from above, while the entire room around you is lit by sunlight filtered through beautiful, custom stained glass windows, the most prominent of which features the magnificent Bavarian Lion, the mascot of Bavaria, rendered as always in Bavarian blue and white. Also, look around more closely, and you'll see the three favorite flowers of Bavarian—*Edelweiss, Enzian*, and *Almenrausch*. Frequent attendance by Bavarian folk dancers and musicians make the Bavarian character

of the dining atmosphere complete.

Classic good taste has earned The Bavarian Inn a reputation for excellence in food and service. While many restaurants follow trends to attract new clientele, the Bavarian Inn stands firm in its traditional cooking. "We have found our customers want authentic German cuisine." explains Cerda. And true to form, the most popular menu item remains Weiner Schnizel.

Indeed, many have hoisted a stein at the annual three weekend Oktoberfest, Wisconsin's oldest and most authentic, held behind the Bavarian Inn in what is known as Heidelberg Park.

Just visiting the Bavarian Inn complex is a unique experience. Enjoying a delicious, carefully-prepared meal can only enhance your time at this Milwaukee landmark.

ROAST DUCK SHANKS WITH DRIED CHERRY/ROSEMARY SAUCE

INGREDIENTS

8 duck shanks lightly seasoned with salt pepper
  and poultry seasoning

2 cups demi glace

2 cups chicken stock

2 sprigs rosemary

1 cup dried cherries (raisins may substitute)

½ cup orange juice

Zest of 1 orange

½ cup red wine

4 cups prepared wild rice

4 cups prepared red cabbage

Season duck shanks with salt, pepper, and poultry seasoning. Heat a large sauté or dutch oven pan on the stove top. Brown duck shanks, add chicken stock, demi-glace, rosemary, orange juice, red wine and orange zest. Bring to a boil and then place in a 300 degree oven for about 1 ½ hrs. Remove from cooking stock and place to the side. Add cherries and reduce cooking stock by half. Salt and pepper to taste. Present with prepared wild rice and red cabbage.

SERVES 4

Pan Seared Venison Medallions with Currant-Green Peppercorn Sauce

Ingredients

2 lbs. venison loin cut into 3 oz. portions

1 can green peppercorns drained and
*   rinsed well*

6 oz. currant jelly

6 oz. veal demi glace

4 sprigs fresh thyme

4 tbls. cold butter

½ cup Cabernet Sauvignon

1 tsp. fresh chopped garlic

4 yellow squash

4 zucchini

Small red potatoes peeled and boiled

Salt and pepper

Heat sauté pan to high temperature. Season medallions with salt and pepper, place in pan with light oil and sear on both sides. Place in 325 degree oven and cook for about six minutes or medium rare. Remove from pan and let rest. Lightly sauté garlic in the same pan, deglaze with red wine, add currant jelly and demi-glace. Reduce by one half. Add peppercorns, thyme and butter.

Cut squash in half and slice on an angle so as to alternate in a pattern. Place on sheet tray to roast or steam (whichever is your preference).

Heat potatoes in a warm pan with butter, salt, pepper, and chopped parsley.

Present venison on top of sauce with vegetables and potatoes.

Serves 4-6

VOLCANO VEAL SHANK
WITH WILD MUSHROOMS

INGREDIENTS

4 - 12 oz. to 16 oz. veal shanks

1 onion diced

2 carrots diced

4 celery ribs diced

4 oz. tomato paste

1 oz. chopped garlic

4 sprigs thyme

4 bay leaves

4 cups chicken or veal stock

4 cups red wine

3 portabella mushrooms sliced

½ lb. shiitake mushrooms sliced

1 cup red wine

1 tsp. chopped garlic

4 asparagus bundles prepared

4 cups prepared braised spiced red cabbage

4 cups prepared spaetzle

The impressive Kachelofen *stands in the lobby of the Bavarian Inn.*

Heat large pot to high heat.

Add ½ cup oil, season veal shanks and brown in pan. Add onions, carrots, celery, garlic, thyme, and bay leaves. Sauté vegetables until lightly cooked. Add tomato paste, wine, and stock. Reduce to a simmer and cook until tender (approx. 1 ½ hrs.) Remove veal and reduce stock by one half. Strain veggies and discard; reserve the jus for later. Sauté mushrooms, add jus and season with salt and pepper.

Present on a bed of sautéed spaetzle, red cabbage and asparagus. Smother veal with mushroom jus.

SERVES 4

BLACK WALNUT TORTE

INGREDIENTS

TORTE CRUST

4 cups flour

1 ½ cups salted butter

1 cup sugar

1 tsp. salt

1 egg yolk

½ cup finely ground black walnuts

FILLING

2 cups coarse ground black walnuts

8 egg yolks

2 ½ cups heavy cream

1 Tbls. vanilla extract

¾ cup sugar

3 Tbls. corn starch

2 cups prepared chocolate ganáche

Prepare crust by combining all dry ingredients including walnuts. Add cold butter and work into dry ingredients until pea size flakes are achieved. Work egg yolk in gently. Roll on a floured surface and size to fit in a greased torte pan. Par bake at 350 degrees for 5 minutes. Set aside to cool.

Prepare filling by combining heavy cream, vanilla, corn starch and sugar in a double boiler pan. Heat to a simmer and then add walnuts. Reduce cream by ¼ or until filling begins to thicken slightly. Add egg yolks and whisk lightly. Remove from heat and pour into prepared pastry crust. Bake at 325 degrees for 40 minutes and cool. Pour warm ganáche over the top and cool. Cut and serve.

SERVES 6 – 8

Karl Ratzsch's

Triumvirate. *Chef John Poulos, Dining Room Manager Judy Hazard, and Restaurant Manager Tom Andera.*

"If any restaurant exemplifies Milwaukee's brand of friendliness, warmth, and spirit, it is Karl Ratzsch's," says Dining Room Manager, Judy Hazard. "At Ratzsch's, we like our guests to feel like we are celebrating the holiday season 365 days of the year." A product of love's labor, the restaurant opened in 1904. Then in 1929, romance bloomed between Helen Herman, a manager at her Uncle Otto Herman's Café and newly hired busboy, Karl Ratzsch. After renaming Herman's café to Karl Ratzsch's, the couple carried on the family business, relocating their restaurant one block east of its original location on Water and Mason streets.

Karl and Helen, affectionately known as "Papa" and "Mama" Ratzsch, continued managing the restaurant until 1962, when Karl Jr. became owner. In early 2003, the story of a busboy's rise to owner would be repeated, with a slight twist. Son Josef sold the restaurant to three long-term employees, Tom Andera, Judy Hazard, and John Poulos. Restaurant Manager Tom Andera started at Ratzsch's as a part-time busser while a student at Marquette University. Together the three, who practically grew up in the restaurant, continue the Ratzsch family's dream of sharing their internationally acclaimed cuisine.

In the weeks before Christmas, Ratzsch's sparkles with carefully hung decorations. Green boughs and festive lights are strung from the beamed ceiling. Families and friends delight in live piano performances of holiday tunes. In the bar area, guests toast their steins and often share a frothy batch of homemade Tom & Jerry's. Patrons cannot miss the photos of the many celebrities and dignitaries, ranging from Bob Hope to Louis Armstrong, who line the walls.

The main dining room is filled with the holiday bustle year-round, as waitresses in Bavarian Dirndl dresses balance a parade of platters heaped with Ratzsch's now famous roasted goose breast, duck, and Wiener Schnitzel. While preserving the Ratzsch family's 1904 recipes, the new owners added lighter German fare to the dinner menu in 1996, including broiled-planked Whitefish filet served with potato bordure and the mermaid's salad. In addition, the management trio now serves up a Friday night fish fry, a Milwaukee culinary custom dating back to the 1800s. The start of the weekend is announced as families, dig into golden, crisp, haddock coated in a Sprecher beer batter and homemade coleslaw and potato pancakes.

The restaurant has received local, regional, and national acclaim over the years, collecting awards from DiRoNA, Wine Spectator, and an Ivy from Restaurants & Institutions, among many others. Karl Jr. is a DiRoNA Hall of Fame member for career excellence.

"Ratzsch's is a place to make memories," says Tom Andera, as he holds up a stein of German lager. "We like to think of our self as a restaurant people go to for entertaining, whether the occasion is business, a wedding, a birthday, or Christmas."

OCTOBERFEST STRUDEL

INGREDIENTS

5 lbs. strained sauerkraut

5 lbs. smoked pork

2 lbs. Swiss cheese

3 oz. melted butter

1 cup cracker meal

DOUGH

1 1/2 lbs. flour, separated

1 1/2 oz. soft butter

1 egg

Pinch of salt

2 1/2 cups warm water

Octoberfest Strudel was Chef John's inspiration about ten years ago. Always looking for different nuances in technique and preparation, he took a time-honored fruit dessert preparation and transformed it into a modern german-style appetizer.

To make the dough, put all ingredients in mixing bowl, except 1 cup of flour. Mix on slow speed with dough hook, adding flour until you have a dough ball effect. The dough should be sticking slightly to mixing bowl.

Take the dough out of the bowl and put on a floured sheet pan, pressing dough down to flatten slightly. Brush with melted butter and let it rest at room temperature for 1/2 hour.

Place a tablecloth on a large six-foot by two-foot table. Spread flour over it, and roll out the dough. Use rolling pin to start and then pull with floured hands to stretch completely over table. Dough should be almost paper thin.

Sprinkle cracker meal evenly across dough. Discard thick ends pieces.

Next add sauerkraut lengthwise across the dough at edge of table and top with smoked pork, Swiss cheese, and butter. Fold the edge over, grabbing tablecloth with two hands and roll tightly, like a jelly roll. Remove strudel from table to heavily floured sheet pan.

Preheat oven to 400 degrees. In a sauté pan heat 3 tablespoons of cooking oil over medium heat. Place a three-inch wide piece strudel in pan and brown on one side, turn over strudel and then drain grease out of pan. Add a touch of melted butter over strudel and make sure smoked pork and Swiss cheese side is up. Bake for 5 min.

SERVES 15 PEOPLE.

ROAST GOOSE SHANKS

In the mid 1950s, the Goose Shank recipe was the star attraction of the legendary $1,000 dinner for Concertmaster Arthur Fiedler which Karl had flown in from Strasbourg. The goose is very patiently roasted and pampered ... literally done to a turn to ensure its tenderness.

INGREDIENTS

4 - 1 lb. goose shanks

2 1/2 qts. hot chicken stock

1 large onion

Flour

1 cup apple slices

Seasoning salt

1 clove garlic

1 bay leaf

Ground white pepper

Sprinkle goose with seasoning salt and white pepper. Place in 4 inch deep roasting pan. Add goose skin side up and place in oven at 350 degrees until slightly browned, about half an hour. Add chicken stock, onions, garlic, bay leaf and apples. Cover and roast until tender, about 3 1/2 hours, reduce oven to 250 degrees, uncover for last half hour. Remove goose to serving dish, skim grease and combine with flour to make a roux in sauce pan. Add strained goose stock and bring to boil until desired thickness. Adjust flavor if needed. Strain gravy and pour over goose shank.

SERVES 4

CRACKLING PORK SHANK

The pork shank has been a favorite in Greman kitchens for centuries. After slow cooking in its own juices, we take the preparation a step further in the crisping process by plunging it into hot oil. This results in a delicious crispy exterior while maintaining a moist succulent interior.

INGREDIENTS

3 lbs. pork shank

3 quarts cooking oil

2 Tbls. kosher salt

Orange rind

Lemon rind

Chili pepper

1 Tbls. pickling spice

In a heavy gauge soup kettle, soak pork shank in salt water overnight. Discard water, then add into the kettle 3 quarts of oil, pork shank, salt, orange rind, lemon rind, chili pepper, and pickling spice. Turn on medium heat until oil reaches 230 degrees, then turn down to low and simmer pork shank about 3 hours until tender. Remove pork shank from oil when done. Place on a paper towel. When ready to serve, strain oil and bring oil temperature up to 350 degrees. Add pork shank and fry until crispy, about 3 minutes. Serve with sauerkraut and potatoes.

SERVES 1

HONEY WALNUT STRUDEL

This dessert blends the honey and cinnamon of Chef John's Greek heritage with traditional German strudel
dough and crushed walnuts. This treat is a delightful fusion of Continental flavors.

INGREDIENTS

DOUGH FOR 48

1 1/2 lbs. flour
1 1/2 oz. soft butter
1 egg
Pinch of salt
2 1/2 cups warm water

FILLING FOR 1

Vanilla ice cream
3 Tbls. honey
Fresh whipped cream
Cinnamon
3 Tbls. toasted walnuts
Powdered sugar

Put all ingredients in mixing bowl, except 1 cup of flour, mix on slow speed with dough hook, adding flour until you have a dough ball effect. Dough should be sticking slightly to mixing bowl.

Take dough out of bowl and put on floured sheet pan, pressing dough down to flatten slightly. Brush with melted butter and allow to rest at room temperature for 1/2 hour.

Heat oil to 350 degrees. Roll 1/2 oz. of dough out on floured table to eighth inch thickness. Place dough in 6 oz. ladle and cover with another ladle to keep its form while deep frying at 350 degrees until light brown in color. Take out and place on a paper towel.

To serve, fill pastry with large scoop of vanilla ice cream and top with chopped toasted walnuts, drizzle with honey, cinnamon and powdered sugar. Garnish with fresh whipped cream.

Mader's Restaurant

Victor Mader, Owner

"Mader's was famous before you and I were born, " says Executive Manager Daniel Hazard. "Our generation's job is to continue that great tradition."

Charles Mader, came to the United States in 1894 from Munich, Germany, with dreams of owning a restaurant. Since the day he first purchased a building on 233 West Water Street (now Plankinton Avenue) and called it "The Comfort," Mader's has continued to grow. As the restaurant expanded over its 104 year history, so has its owner's dream.

The Comfort, as Mader's was formerly named, opened its doors during a time when the dinner bill totaled twenty cents and large steins of frothy "Cream City" beer cost three shiny pennies. In those early years, the Comfort lived up to its humble name. Mader's current collection of Germanic weaponry, early Mettlach steins, beautiful European-style wood carvings, and stained glass windows were still decades away from arriving.

After meeting success, the Comfort moved to its present location on Old World Third Street. When Prohibition was announced, Mader averted potential disaster by focusing on German recipes, perfecting dishes that today receive national acclaim. George and Gustave took over full-time management of their father's business operations in 1938. The family tradition continued in 1964, when Gustave's son, Victor, joined the establishment.

Over the years, Mader's has maintained a loyal and ever-growing customer base. "Everyone who comes through our doors knows that they are welcome," insists owner Victor Mader. "For 104 years, we have provided a memorable dining experience."

Much of Mader's success is due to its beloved rustic German cuisine and to the staff's attention to detail. While the recipes are simple, preparation is meticulous. "Our Sauerbraten, for example, is marinated in a red wine vinegar with pickling spice and onions," says Mader "The secret ingredient is the care, personal attention, and spirit in which each dish is prepared."

Over the years, Mader's has played host to celebrities and statesmen alike. Cary Grant, Audrey Hepburn, and Paul Newman came in for the Mader's experience. American Presidents Truman, Kennedy, Reagan, and Ford, and even Mexican President Vicente Fox enjoyed Mader's finest dishes. Among the restaurant's many achievements, Mader's was ranked "Best Ethnic Restaurant" by the *Milwaukee Journal-Sentinel*, *Wisconsin Trails*, *Readers of the Shepard Express, Milwaukee Magazine* and *Exclusively Yours*. The popularity of Mader's Viennese Brunch, served every Sunday, was evident when it had to turn away crowds on its opening day in November 1977.

Synonymous with excellent German food, Mader's has become a landmark in downtown Milwaukee. Enhanced by the creative talent of Executive Chef Shawn Monroe, Mader's is a must-see and a must-eat for tourists and locals alike. "We take great pride in selecting the finest ingredients and staff, and in creating the best atmosphere," says Monroe. "We are dedicated to keeping Charles Mader's dream alive by continually delighting our guests' senses."

WIENER SCHNITZEL

Wiener Schnitzel is a veal fillet served Viennese style. It is the most famous traditional dish in Austria. In 1998, Victor Mader discovered a very special breading that Mader's uses to achieve our unique schnitzel. This schnitzel has been on our menue since 1919.

INGREDIENTS

1 lb. veal cutlets

Salt and black pepper

3 eggs beaten

1 cup half-and-half cream

1/4 cup buttermilk

1 cup all-purpose flour

1 cup dry bread crumbs

2 oz. oil

Preheat oven to 250 degrees. Place cutlets between two sheets of plastic wrap and pound to 1/8 inch thickness. Season the cutlets with salt and black pepper to taste.

Combine the eggs, buttermilk, and half-and-half.

Dredge the cutlets in flour, shaking off any excess. Dip the cutlet in egg mixture, allowing the extra to drain off before coating the cutlets with the bread crumb mixture.

Fry cutlets in oil until they are golden brown. Then place them in the oven for five to seven minutes. Serve with a lemon wedge.

SERVES 4

WILD BOAR EN CROUTE

Wild boar is perhaps the oldest of German dishes, dating back thousands of years. Traditionally captured in the Black Forest area of Germany, these wily and dangerous animals are used to create a sought after and very flavorful German sausage.

INGREDIENTS

2 - 4 oz. wild boar sausages

2 - 4 in. x 4 in. puff pastry sheets

1/2 Tbls. butter

1/2 cup chopped button mushrooms

1 Tbls. chopped shallots

1 tsp. garlic

Pinch of thyme

2 Tbls. sherry wine

1/4 cup heavy cream

1 egg

Fully cook the wild boar sausages in a skillet, or grill them as preferred. Allow the sausages to cool completely.

In a pan, sauté chopped mushrooms until the liquid has evaporated. Add shallots and continue to cook for three to five minutes. Add the garlic and continue to cook for an additional minute. Add thyme just before deglazing the pan with sherry wine.

Cook the mixture until the liquid is reduced by half. Add heavy cream and reduce until the mixture is thick, then allow it to cool.

On a cutting board, lay the squares of puff pastry and brush with egg wash. Place 1 tablespoon of the mixture on each square. Place one sausage on the mixture diagonally. Completely wrap the sausage with the puff pastry and brush with egg wash.

Bake the two stuffed pastries at 400 degrees for 15 minutes, or until golden brown.

Cut on the bias, just before plating the sausages and serve with loganberry preserves.

SERVES 2

ROAST PORK SHANK

Roast Pork Shank has been our most unique and famous dish for over 100 years. We have served this renowned German meal for 99 years with the "skin on." Our shank is butter tender and served with barrel-cured sauerkraut.

INGREDIENTS

2 - 18 oz. pork shanks

Oil for searing

1/2 medium onion sliced

1 small carrot

1 rib celery

2 red apples chopped

Apple cider

All-purpose flour

Salt and black pepper, to taste

Season pork shanks with salt and black pepper on all sides to taste. In a large roasting pan, sear the pork shanks in hot oil on all sides.

Add onion, carrot, celery, chopped apples to the pan. Roast these ingredients lightly.

Deglaze the roasting pan with apple cider and a small amount of water. Cover the roasting pan and bake for 45 minutes to 1 hour at 375 degrees.

Uncover the pan and continue to roast the dish for an additional 30 to 45 minutes. After removing the shanks and vegetables, make a gravy from the drippings.

SERVES 2

CRÈME BRÛLÉE

Crème Brûlée translates from French as burnt cream. It is a dessert consisting of a rich custard base topped with a layer of hard caramel, created by burning sugar under intense heat. Our traditional dessert is vanilla flavored and served in a cold ramekin.

INGREDIENTS

8 egg yolks

1-3/4 cups heavy cream

1/2 vanilla bean

1/3 cup sugar

1 oz. dry sifted brown sugar

Separate eight egg yolks from the whites and place the yolks in a stainless mixing bowl with 1/3 cup of sugar.

Heat 1-3/4 cups of heavy cream in a stainless saucepan, adding the vanilla as the mixture heats.

When the cream starts to simmer, temper the egg mixture with 1/3 of the hot cream. Mix well and add the egg/cream mixture back to the saucepan. Continue to cook the mixture for 5 additional minutes. Double strain this mixture and chill over ice.

After mixture cools, pour into ramekins (about 2/3 full). Place ramekins in large pan and pour water around ramekins half the way up and bake at 325 degrees for 15-20 minutes.

Before serving sprinkle brown sugar evenly over the top of the crème brûlée and caramelize using a broiler oven.

SERVES 16

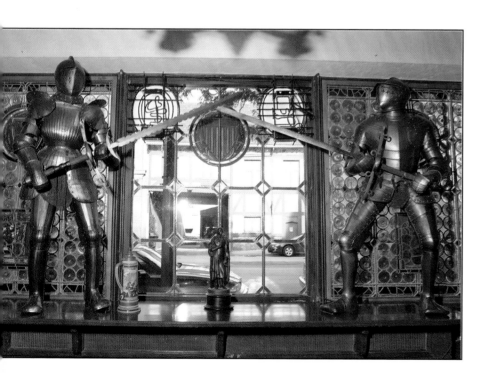

Weissgerber's Gasthaus

Hans and Maria Weissgerber

"Our family is very fortunate and proud to share in the American Dream," says Ramona Weissgerber-Kummer, general manager of *Weissgerber's Gasthaus.* Opening their first family restaurant in 1967, Hans and Maria Weissgerber emigrated 11 years earlier from the Black Forest area, a densely wooded mountain region tucked away in the southwestern corner of the Germany.

Starting with nothing, the Weissgerbers accomplished more than they thought possible. Hans and Maria started work in South Bend, Indiana, where Hans worked for Volpano's Pizzeria. His highlight was meeting Marilyn Monroe as he was tossing pizza dough. Although he could not speak fluent English, he was able to steal a kiss from her. After connecting with relatives from the Old Country, Hans learned that they had many friends in the Milwaukee area, thus settling there in 1956. Hans quickly found a job as sausage maker for Uncle August Sausage Company and then a meat cutter and a cook at the Milwaukee Elk's Club.

With the help of their sons, Hans Jr. and Jack, the first Weissgerber Restaurant, the Golden Mast on Okauchee Lake opened in 1967 and then the Seven Seas on Lake Nagawicka in 1981. The popularity of their first two restaurants fueled bigger dreams of bringing Old World cuisine and charm to Milwaukee's New World palates.

Emulating the country inns of villages and towns in Germany, *Weissgerber's Gasthaus* opened in 1983, returning Milwaukee residents to a time when the city's best restaurants were German. Upon entering the Gasthaus, guests are transported from the bustling streets of Waukesha to the romantic countryside of Southern Germany or Austria.

Patrons are greeted by waitresses in Bavarian *dirndl* dresses, and waiters suited with *edelweiss* ties greet patrons. They can choose to dine in one of four uniquely themed rooms, including the Bavarian-style main dining room.

"My grandparents were proud to share their culture and traditions with guests," says Ramona Weissgerber-Kummer. "We keep the recipes they selected as true to the day they opened." The dinner selection offers authentic German recipes such as *Opa* Weissgerber's pork shank, cured for almost a week until moist and then roasted crisp, and our famous sauerbraten, which is marinated in select spices and red wine for 7-10 days.

These specialties are expertly prepared by chefs who have been loyal to the Weissgerber family for many years. Recent offerings on the menu include lighter and more modern dishes, such as the popular Black Forest's chop salad and sesame crusted salmon bites. Giant Barvarian pretzels and big steins of beer make the Biergarten and Bar a fun place to meet up with friends and business associates.

"The Bavarian spirit is to treat our customers like long lost family," insists Ramona. "We put out our best dishes, prepare the best food, and share the best drinks." A statue of King Gambrinus, the patron saint of beer, presides in the lounge as guests sip the specially brewed Weissgerber Amber House Beer. Stained glass windows allow a soft light to shine through handmade tapestries. The massive stone fireplace on the west wall warms guests on chilly winter evenings. Paintings depicting castles along the Rhine adorn the room's high walls. Best described as rich, yet honest, Weissgerber *Gasthaus*' refined ambience is matched by rustic, delightful fare. Road-weary travelers and locals alike are welcome to rest and enjoy a unique dining experience with that touch of *Gemütlichkeit*.

Now retired, Hans Sr. stops by once in a while to visit with customers and friends. "Our traditions are strengthened by the commitment to family," attest Hans. "My sons own the restaurant now. They are encouraging a third generation to preserve the German tradition of good food, beer and wine and old fashioned hospitality.

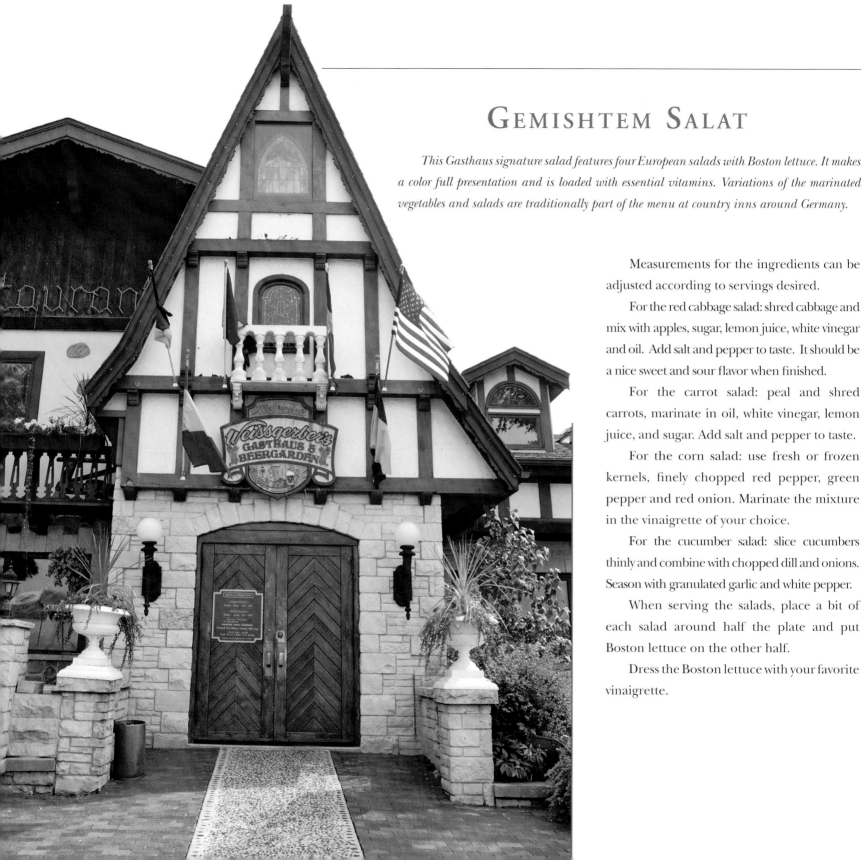

Gemishtem Salat

This Gasthaus signature salad features four European salads with Boston lettuce. It makes a color full presentation and is loaded with essential vitamins. Variations of the marinated vegetables and salads are traditionally part of the menu at country inns around Germany.

Measurements for the ingredients can be adjusted according to servings desired.

For the red cabbage salad: shred cabbage and mix with apples, sugar, lemon juice, white vinegar and oil. Add salt and pepper to taste. It should be a nice sweet and sour flavor when finished.

For the carrot salad: peal and shred carrots, marinate in oil, white vinegar, lemon juice, and sugar. Add salt and pepper to taste.

For the corn salad: use fresh or frozen kernels, finely chopped red pepper, green pepper and red onion. Marinate the mixture in the vinaigrette of your choice.

For the cucumber salad: slice cucumbers thinly and combine with chopped dill and onions. Season with granulated garlic and white pepper.

When serving the salads, place a bit of each salad around half the plate and put Boston lettuce on the other half.

Dress the Boston lettuce with your favorite vinaigrette.

WÜRSTCHEN

These small bites of sausage entice the palate of everyone who tries them. The sausage, peppers, and kraut get the appetite geared up for a great meal. Serve with a good German mustard and Bavarian style beer to match.

INGREDIENTS

1 lb. Sauerkraut - may add sautéed onions, caraway, white wine, and brown sugar to taste

1 red pepper

1 yellow pepper

1 green pepper

1 red onion

4 Knackwurst

4 Bauern Bratwurst (Or any type of sausage you like)

Ground black pepper

Cut peppers and onion into pieces, season with salt and freshly ground black pepper. Lightly saute mixture in olive oil.

Heat sauerkraut in oven at 350 degrees for 20 minutes.

Cook sausage in a sauce pan with water for about 10 minutes. Slice sausage into 3 to 4 pieces. Skewer pepper, sausage and onions alternately.

Place a helping of sauerkraut on each serving plate and top with 1 to 2 skewers.

SERVES 8

SCHNITZEL A LA HOLSTEIN

Garnishing with caviar, lachs, toast points and anchovy is the original preparation for Germany's famous diplomats von Holstein and Furst von Bismarck, thus the name Schintzel a la Holstein.

INGREDIENTS

14 oz. of veal (scallopini cut)

3 eggs beaten with 3 tbls. water

1 cup bread crumbs

1 cup flour

4 sunny-side-up fried eggs

4 anchovy filets

*2 pieces of white bread – toasted and
      sliced into 4 triangles each*

4 slices of lachs (salmon)

Caviar to garnish

Select 3 to 4 oz portions of veal. Cover with plastic wrap and firmly flatten with a meat tenderizer, approximately 1/4 inch thick

Lightly season with salt and white pepper, followed by a standard breading procedure.

The basic steps to breading schnitzels is to dust with flour, dip in egg wash (3 eggs beaten with 3 tablespoons of water) and cover with bread crumbs.

Saute Schnitzel in a nonstick pan in oil until golden brown, about 3 minutes on each side, being careful not to overcook it. The cutlet should remain moist and tender on the inside.

Place 2 pieces of schnitzel on a serving platter and garnish the top with Sunny side up egg, anchovy and toast points topped with caviar and lachs.

This dish is typically paired with pan fried potatoes. Schnitzel can be served with out the garnishes or with slice of lemon.

SERVES 3 TO 4

SCHWARZWÄLDER KIRSCHTORTE

This unusual blend of chocolate, cherries, Kirsch, whipped cream, and shaved chocolate is a specialty throughout Swabia. There are many variations on this theme, but this recipe tastes and looks wonderful. It can be served with a glass of Kirschwasser for a special touch.

INGREDIENTS

1 box white cake mix – follow package directions except replace ¼ cup water with ¼ rum
1 box chocolate cake mix – follow package directions

CHERRY FILLING

1 can cherry pie filling
1 can dark sweet cherries – drained
3 Tbls. Kirschwasser
1 tsp. Knox gelatin
1/8 cup boiling water

CHOCOLATE FROSTING

4 oz. butter softened
½ oz. unsweetened chocolate melted
½ oz. dark rum
2/3 cup powdered sugar

TOPPING

2 half pints Rich's whip topping – not creamer
¼ tsp. vanilla extract
¼ tsp. almond extract
Powdered sugar to taste
Chocolate shavings
Maraschino cherries

Mix gelatin with boiling water and cool, then add to the other combined filling ingredients. Let set overnight.

Whip ingredients until fluffy and have at room temperature when assembling the cake.

Whip topping until thick. Flavor with vanilla & almond extracts and sugar, chill.

Bake both cake mixes using 10 inch greased spring form pans. Cool and cut the top off of both to make a flat surface. Cut each layer in half.

Order of assembly:
• chocolate cake layer
• chocolate frosting
• 1/2 cherry filling – 1 inch from edge
• pipe cream around edge to fill in
• white cake layer
• remaining cherry filling – 1 inch from edge
• pipe cream around edge to fill in
• chocolate layer
• whipped topping

At this point score the cake using a knife into 16 sections.

Add rosettes of whipped topping, chocolate shavings, and Maraschino cherries.

(You will have one white cake layer left over, which can be frozen for future use.)

SERVES 16

THE LAST 50 YEARS

When we think of "German" we think of the "modern" European country bordered today by Austria, Switzerland, France, Belgium, Holland, Poland, Slovenia, and the Czech Republic. However, when the term "German" is used, it really includes all German-speakers.

The last 50 years have seen a decline in the German presence in Milwaukee. The Milwaukee Turners is the only remaining German building that has seen constant use for the same purpose: social activities, fitness and restaurant. Many shopping districts catering to "German" customers no longer exist. However, there are businesses which promote the stereotypical aspects of what has become known as "German": steins, sausage, Hummels.

Just like the early immigrants came together for fellowship, later arrivals, too, joined or formed clubs. These clubs not only teach the old dances and songs, they also teach the younger generations about their ancestral traditions. The Pomeranians have their club house with a library and an extensive genealogy service; a *Pommern Tag* picnic each June; and rehearsal space for the Freistadt Alte Kameraden Band.

Germantown (23 miles west of downtown Milwaukee) is a prime illustration of a community emphasizing its German heritage. The city's welcome sign reads *Willkommen* and the parks have German names. Even the architecture of the strip malls is German-inspired. In addition, a Germantown grocery store features permanent department signs in German and neighborhood specialty stores offer German fare. Further, the local *Hessischer Verein* (Hessen Club) holds an annual *Mai Fest*.

Germantown has made a real effort to identify itself with "Old World" Germany.

However, links to the city's German heritage can be found all around Milwaukee. The Carl Schurz Memorial Park in Stone Bank holds an annual German American Day each August. The United Donauschwaben has its own *Schwabenhof* in Menomonee Falls. Milwaukee Public Schools has a German Immersion School; *Die Volkshochschule* holds German language classes; the *Kulturvereinigung* conducts Saturday German classes for children; and the Goethe House has classes for adults as well as summer *Kinder Kamps* for children. For those interested in stamp collections, the Germany Philatelic Society holds monthly meetings.

Oktoberfests are popular at the Bavarian Inn, the *Schwabenhof* in Menomonee Falls, and in West Bend. The *Rheinischer Verein* and the Bavarian Soccer Club hold annual *Fasching* (Mardi Gras) celebrations. German Radio Programs, which include the Continental Showcase, *Stimmungs Stunde*, and *Melodien von Deutschland Donauschwäbische Heimatklänge*, which all air weekly.

Ozaukee County Historical Society's Pioneer Village (30 miles north) is 90% German. The village contains 20 restored and authentically furnished houses, barns and outbuildings, all of which show how immigrant Germans lived in the 1800s.

There are traces of Milwaukee's German background in even newly-established enterprises. The *Blumen Markt* is a flower shop in the recently developed Public Market. Everyone uses German words such as *delicatessen, stein, kindergarten, hausfrau,*

sauerkraut, pumpernickel, tannenbaum, and *frankfurter,* among many others.

Many originally German names have been anglicized over the years. Some examples are Schneider to Taylor; Mueller to Miller; Bäcker to Baker; and Schmidt to Smith. The most common German names in the Milwaukee telephone directory are variations on Maier: Meier, Mier, Meyer, Mayer, Maher, Meagher, etc. There are 1,650 listed. The Milwaukee telephone directory also has more names beginning with "Sch" (15,650) than the Munich, Germany directory. Of those, variations on Schmidt number 2,400.

Change is all around us. There are some continuations and some new versions of old themes; there are some new innovations and improvements, but today, sadly, we no longer can go "Down by Schuster's," but we can still drink Grandpa Graf's Root Beer. There are fewer and fewer remaining German butcher shops, bakeries, and restaurants downtown, but we do have our fond memories.

According to the 1990 United States Census Bureau statistics, Wisconsin is the most "German" of all states with 56 per cent of the Wisconsin population claiming German-speaking heritage. Throughout the last few decades, there has been a resurgence of pride in German ancestry. Just as the infrastructure of Milwaukee is undergoing a revitalization, attitudes about Germans, German heritage, and German contributions are also undergoing a renaissance. Germans need to preserve yesterday's heritage for tomorrow. This will ensure Milwaukee's reputation continues as "A Great Place on a Great Lake."

MILWAUKEE-AREA GERMAN ORGANIZATIONS TODAY

American Historical Society of Germans from Russia
Apatiner Club
Aurora Lodge #30 F&AM
Austrian-American Society
Bavarian Soccer Club
Bayerischer Vergnügungs Club
Berliner Bären
Carl Schurz Memorial Park
Club Eichenlaub
D.A.N.K.
Danube Cultural Society of Southeastern Wisconsin
Deutsch-Amerikanisher Schützen Club
Deutscher Sprach & Schulverein
D'Holzhacker Buam
D'Lustig'n Wendlstoana
German American Societies
German Fest Milwaukee, Inc.
Germany Philatelic Society
Gesang Verein Bavaria
Goethe House of Wisconsin
Hessischer Verein
Klub der Pommern Inc.
Kulturvereinigung und Deutsche Schule
Max Kade Institute
Milwaukee Damenchor
Milwaukee Donauschwaben
Milwaukee Liederkranz
Milwaukee Liedertafel
Milwaukee Sport Club
Milwaukee Turnverein
Musci Family Club
Muller Fasching Verein Nordamerika, Inc.
Pommersche Tanzdeel Freistadt
Pommerscher Verein Freistadt
RheinischerVerein Grün Weiss
S.V.E.V. D'Oberlandler
Schlaraffia
Schlesier Verein
Schwaben Männerchor
Schwaben Unterstützungsverein
Spielmannszug Milwaukee
United German Societies of Milwaukee, Inc.
United German Choruses of Milwaukee
Wisconsin Sängerbezirk

Sprecher Brewery in Glendale, a local brewery, produces a variety of beers and sodas. Although several micro-breweries are in existance, Sprecher, with Lakefront Brewery and Miller Brewing Company, are the three remaining breweries in Milwaukee.

New on the block, but old in tradition, The Old German Beer Hall on Old World Third Street provides a warm and friendly atmosphere, reminiscent of the Hofbräu Haus in Munich, Germany.

At the beautiful Blatz Temple of Music in Washington Park, the fine tradition of presenting concerts and theatrical performances continues throughout the summer months. The Goethe-Schiller monument faces this band shell across the green.

Ernst von Falkenberg demonstrated blacksmithing at the Cultural Exhibition of a recent German Fest.

This group is one of the Donau-Schwaben *(Danube Swabians) dance groups which perpetuate German dance and tradition of their region.*

Dieter Damrow, president of the Schwaben Männerchor; Frank Schmitz, president of the United German Choruses of Milwaukee; and Rolf Hoffmann, then president of the Wisconsin Sängerbezirk admire an award.

Santa's elves, from the organization From the Hart, usher in the holiday season with a jolly concert at the Pabst Mansion.

This volunteer, one of 4000 at the Wisconsin Holiday Folk Fair, staffs the German Bakery Booth. The Folk Fair began in 1943 and is the oldest and largest multi-ethnic festival of its type in the country. It showcases cultures, through food, music, dance, history, unique crafts, and holiday gifts. Visitors can learn to say "Hello!" in dozens of languages.

The Vereinigte Männerchöre *(United German Choruses at Milwaukee) perform at Mount Mary College in Milwaukee at an annual Christmas Concert. The group is made up of five active choruses which delight the audience with timeless favorites.*

This Bavarian Dance Group performs on stage at the Holiday Folk Fair, along with many other ethnic groups. The Schuplattler *group hops, claps, and slaps while dancing to the beat of the Alpine music played on the accordion.*

Harold Schoessow takes a break from his performance with the Alte Kamaraden, *a local brass band founded in 1942, which continues to entertain in the greater Milwaukee area.*

German Fest Milwaukee, Inc. was formed at the urging of Mayor Henry Maier in 1980. Volunteers of 44 German-speaking organizations in the Milwaukee area produce this colorful annual three-day festival on the Summerfest Grounds at Lake Michigan's shore. The Fest provides excellent food, satisfying beverages, and delectable desserts for the palate; exciting entertainment and incredible shops with every imaginable German item (and then some!); and a cultural exhibition and a gala parade showcasing traditional regional German ethnic clothing. German Fest organizers transport guests into a "homeland reverie" and contribute to the *Gemütlichkeit* (good time) a visitor experiences at the Fest. The annual German Fest on Milwaukee's beautiful lakefront is the largest three-day German festival in the United States.

A Bavarian dance group in the German Fest Parade (above).

Dancers from the Pommerscher Tanzdeel Freistadt *(right).*

Three happy parade participants (left); two on the left are from the Pommerscher Tanzdeel Freistadt.

CONTRIBUTORS

Anderson, Kent
Barber, Rose Marie
Bethke, Gerald
Broeniman, Barbara
Brumder, E. J.
Buzard, Barbara and Donald
Casterline, Sandy
Coleman, Jacqueline
Eastberg, John
Eschweiler, Gabi and Tom
Gallun, Dorothy
Gallun, John T.
German Fest Milwaukee, Inc.
Grace Lutheran Church
Haese, Elfrieda

Hatala, Carlen
Hoffmann, Rolf
Holiday Folk Fair International
Kent, Rachel
Kraft, Elaine
Krause III, Charles
Lawent, Melissa
Lindemann, Jean
Lindemann, Rickey
Messer, Traudl
Milwaukee County Historical
  Society
Max Kade Institute
Milwaukee Public Library
Milwaukee Turners

Mueller, Rudy
Nunnemacher, Hermann
Old World Wisconsin
Ozaukee County Historical Society
  – Pioneer Village
Palmer, Virginia A.
Paradis-Kent, M. Robin
Paradis, Trudy Knauss
Preston, Laurie
Rittenhouse, Carol
Rosing, Gretchen
Schmidt, R. C.
Schmitz, Linda
Schultz, FloryAnn
Schweitzer, Fanny Binter

Seidel, Fritz
Seidel, Stephen
Sherman Park Lutheran Church
Uhle, Karen
University of Wisconsin-Milwaukee,
  Golda Meir Library, Archives
Usinger, Debra
Vilter, Peter
Volk, Clarence
Vogel III, Fred
Yewer, Marge
Zeidler, Frank

REFERENCES

Ackerman, Sandra. *Milwaukee Then and Now.* 2004.
Aderman, Ralph. *Trading Post to Metropolis.* 1987.
Anello, Arthur P. *An Eclectic History of Milwaukee.* 1983.
Austin, H. Russell. *The Milwaukee Story – the Making of an American City.* 1946.
Biersach, Bill. *Pine Lake Yacht Club Centennial 1890-1990.* 1990.
Bruce, William G. *History of Milwaukee, City and County.* 1922/1997.
Brumder, Herbert. *The Life Story of George and Henriette Brumder.* 1960.
Buck, Diane M and Virginia A. Palmer. *Outdoor Sculpture in Milwaukee.* 1995.
Caspar & Zahn. *Die Stadt Milwaukee Führer.* 1886.
Conard, Howard. *History of Milwaukee from its First Settlement to the Year 1895.* 1895/1997.
Conzen, Kathleen N. *"The German Athens" Milwaukee and the Accommodation of Its Immigrants 1836-1860.* 1972.
Corenthal, Michael G. *The Illustrated History of Wisconsin Music 1840-1990.* 1991.
Crowley, Betty. *Stalag Wisconsin.* 2002.
Davis, Susan Burdick. *Wisconsin Lore.* 1931.
Deutschland 1683-1983 U.S. of America. 1983.

Frank, Louis. *Musical Reminiscences on the Cultural Life of Old Milwaukee.* 1979.
Galicich, Anne. *The German Americans.* 1996.
Garber, Randy. *Built in Milwaukee: An Architectural View of the City.* 1984.
Gregory, John. *History of Milwaukee.* 1931.
Gregory, John. *History of Milwaukee Illustrated.* 1930.
Gurda, John. *Change at the River Mouth : Ethnic Succession on Milwaukee's Jones Island, 1700-1922.* 1978.
Gurda, John. *The Making of Milwaukee.* 1999.
Henderson, Speerschneider, and Ferslev. *It Happened Here: Stories of Wisconsin.* 1949.
Kriehn, Ruth. *The Fisherfolk of Jones Island.* 1988.
Lachner, Bert. *Milwauke – Wisconsin: Heimat in the Heartland.* 1995.
Magazine of the Milwaukee County Historical Society. *Milwaukee History.* Autumn, 1987; September, 1968; Spring, 1991.
Manegold, Robert. *Granbob's Memories.* 1995.
Mayer, George. *A Brief History of the Mayerei.* 1990.
Merrill, Peter C. *German-American Artists in Early Milwaukee.* 1997.
Merrill, Peter C. *German-American Urban Culture: Writers and Theaters in Early Milwaukee.* 2000.

Mueller, Theodore. "Milwaukee's German Heritage." *Historical Messenger of the Milwaukee County Historical Society.*
Notable Men of Wisconsin 1901-1902. 1902.
Palmer, Virginia Alice. *Ethnic Sites in Milwaukee County.* 1981.
Pape, Alan. *A Visitor's Guide to Wisconsin's Ethnic Settlement Trail.* 1993.
Prestor, Richard. *Images of America – Milwaukee, Wisconsin.* 2000.
Reiman, Roy. *I Could Write a Book.* 2005.
Rippley, LaVern. *Of German Ways.* 1970.
Uihlein, Erwin. *Autobiography.* 1963.
Van Antwerpen, Louise. *Captain Pabst and the Grand Army of the Republic.* 2005.
"Walk in the City – Historic Walking Tour of Milwaukee's South Side." 1981.
Wells, Robert. *The Milwaukee Journal 1882-1982.* 1982.
Yenowine, George. *Milwaukee, Illustrated New Annual. 1892-1893.* 1893.
Zeitlin, Richard H. *Germans in Wisconsin.* 2000.
Zimmerman, H. Russell. *The Architecture of Eugene Liebert.* 2006.
Zimmerman, H. Russell. *The Heritage Guidebook.* 1989.

ACKNOWLEDGEMENTS

When asked to participate in the production of *German Milwaukee: Its History – Its Recipes*, I hesitated momentarily, then embraced the idea with the deep conviction that this book is truly necessary. We need to know and understand our roots; we need to not only acknowledge but also embrace our heritage! To that end, this book was conceived and completed.

I am extremely grateful to my parents for giving me a proud, positive "take" on being German. I am also grateful to all those who supported this vision and helped to make it a reality.

In particular, E. J. Brumder gave valuable insights, stories and memorabilia. Without his contributions, the book would certainly not be what it is. I am forever in his debt.

Our research and findings was limited to Milwaukee, city and county. If a person or group was inadvertently overlooked or omitted, we can only apologize and hope it will inspire someone else to tell another aspect of this fascinating story.

Thank you to the Milwaukee Turners for sponsoring the project, providing work space, and for Executive Director Rose Marie Barber's efforts in making this book a reality. I am saddened that her untimely death prevented her from seeing this project to completion.

Due to the pictorial layout of this book, space was limited and all materials researched, viewed, and submitted, unfortunately, could not be included. We thank the Milwaukee Public Library and the Milwaukee County Historical Society for preserving photos; for categorizing and cataloging them; and for making them available to us. Special thanks to Steve Daily, Curator of Research Collections at the Historical Society and Tom Olson, Photo Librarian at the Library for skillfully guiding us through their substantial collections.

A heartfelt appreciation goes to those individuals who took the time to save and donate their family photographs to the Historical Society – and a plea to all those with pictures: please label, date, and comment on each picture! If you have photos, do not throw them away – donate them!

To all the contributors of the recipes, we are confident our readers will enjoy both your family stories as well as delectable dishes. They will certainly add flavor to the entire book! We thank you for sharing your family traditions. It is especially gratifying to have the German restaurants in Milwaukee share recipes and history.

My deepest appreciation goes to my daughter, Robin, without whose diligence and determination, this book would not have been published. I would also like to thank my son in law, David, and granddaughter, Rachel, who graciously allowed us and the book "parts" to take over their computer room, dining room, and lives. Thank you for your patience!

We sincerely thank Brad Baraks of G. Bradley Publishing, Inc. for his invaluable assistance. He came from St. Louis regularly to meet with us and prod us, and commit us to producing a great book. We followed his advice and are very grateful for his guidance. Without him, this book certainly would not have come to light.

Researching for this book revealed to me just how pivotal and vital a role the visionary immigrant Germans played in the founding and development of Milwaukee. We are indebted to the early settlers for not seeking a "greener valley" but for settling and staying right here.

PHOTO CREDITS

We would like to thank the following public and commercial contributors for providing photographs used in this book. Many of the images used were from private collections and we would like to express our appreciation to them as well. We would be poorly served and informed without the worthwhile efforts of these groups to preserve and record the images and history of the German community in Milwaukee.

Melissa Lawent; page 211A.
E. J. Brumder Collection; various images.
Milwaukee Turners; numerous images.

Usinger's; pages 66A, 67A
Milwaukee Public Library; pages 12L, 23L, 25R, 27R, 30R, 39TR/BR, 53TL/BL, 56TR/TL, 57TR, 58T/B, 59TR, 62TL/BR, 63TR/BL, 96T, 104A, 106A, 107TL/B, 111TR/BR, 112B, 113TL, 115R, 124B, 130TL, 134BR, 137BR, 148BR, 165TR/BR/LM, 166TL/BL/TR
Milwaukee County Historical Society; pages 8R, 11A, 15B, 16A, 17A, 18A, 19A, 20R/B, 23R, 24A, 25L/B, 26R, 27L, 30L/T, 31B, 34LL, 35L, 37A, 39BL, 41T/BR, 42TL/BL/R, 43A, 44L/M, 45A, 46A, 50A, 51A, 52A, 53RM, 54A, 55TR/B, 56BL, 57L/BR, 59TL/B, 60A, 61A, 64TR, 65BL, 92A, 93A, 94T/R, 96BL/BR, 97TR/BR, 98A, 99M, 100A, 101A, 102A, 103A, 105TR/BR, 107TL, 113BR, 114A, 116A, 117A, 118A, 119TR/BL, 120A, 121A, 122A, 124L, 125A, 126A, 130BL, 131BL/TR, 133A, 134L/TR, 135A, 136A, 137BL, 140R, 142A, 143A, 144A, 146TL/R, 148TL, 149TL, 150TR, 151A, 152A, 153A, 154A, 155T, 156BL/BR, 157A, 158A, 159TR, 160A, 161TL/B, 162A, 163A, 164BL/BR

EPILOGUE

While the Germans were not the first ethnic group to settle in Milwaukee, nor were they the first to begin businesses here, the Germans have always had a knack for seeing what needed to be done and the determination to attempt to improve it. Many times they were successful. They were not the first to brew, but they became the best at brewing, and Miller Brewery is an outstanding example of longevity of German entrepreneurial vision.

From 1870 to the turn of the century, Milwaukee was intensely German in feeling and expression. Milwaukee was *eine schoene deutsche Stadt in Amerika* (a pretty German city in America). Germans were highly regarded as industrious when it came to making their way, and honest when it came to promptly paying their debts. In the early years they were not successful in politics because they did not possess English language skills. Their inability to be successful politicians, however, did not conflict with their sense of duty. Milwaukee Germans were never indifferent to their civic duties, often serving on common councils and various official boards and commissions. Their efforts helped to develop one of the best systems of municipal government and administration in the United States. The Milwaukee-based Socialist Party's endeavors culminated in the development of the national Social Security and Workman's Compensation Systems.

The influence of the Germans in Milwaukee is so great that it affected the entire tenor of the city. The City Hall, the Central Public Library, the Pfister Hotel, and the Pabst Theater and mansion are fine examples of German-influenced architecture. The German singing societies, theaters, and artists all left their marks on this city. The war years saw a great change in attitude toward German affiliations. The pride of "German-ness" which had graced the city for so many years suddenly disappeared. But as the 1990 Federal Census revealed, with 56 percent of Wisconsin residents claiming German-speaking ancestry, that sense of being German had not died, but rather, had just remained quiet for a very long time.

Happily, recent decades have found that sleeping German soul awakening, with a smile, from its decades-long nap. Today, the German-Americans of Milwaukee are not only feeling German, but are also living "German-ness" this time for all the world to see. German-American Milwaukeeans are expressing their heritage through their language, food, dance, culture, and most of all, through their love of Milwaukee. Milwaukee is the city their German-speaking ancestors braved the stormy North Atlantic to reach; the city upon which those ancestors bestowed the best that was "German;" the city, which due in great part to the contributions of many generations of German-Americans, is one that today opens its arms of *Willkommen* to people from from every nation on earth.

Auf Weiderssehen • • • • • • • • • • • *Tschüs!*